In Search of Shadows

Conversations with Egyptian Women

Wédad Zénié-Ziegler

Zed Books
London and New Jersey

In Search of Shadows: Conversations with Egyptian Women was first
published in English by Zed Books Ltd., 57 Caledonian Road,
London
N1 9BU, UK, and 171 First Avenue, Atlantic Highlands,
New Jersey 07716, USA, in 1988.
Originally published in French as *La Face violée des Femmmes d'Egypte*
by Le Mercure de France in 1985.

Cover design Andrew Corbett
Cover picture Mark Edwards
Typeset by AKM Associates (UK) Ltd., Southall, London
Printed and bound in the UK
at The Bath Press, Avon

British Library Cataloguing in Publication Data
Zénié-Ziegler, Wédad
    In search of shadows: conversations with Egyptian women.
    1. Egypt. Society. Role of women
    I. Title   II. La face voilée des femmes d'Egypt. English
    305.4'2'0962

    ISBN 0-86232-806-3
    ISBN 0-86232-807-1 pbk

Library of Congress Cataloging-in-Publication Data
Zénié-Ziegler, Wédad, *1940–*
    [Face violée des femmes d'Egypte.   English]
    In search of shadows: Egyptian women / Wédad Zénié-Ziegler:
    translated by Bob Cumming.
    144p.   cm.
    Translation of: La face voilée des femmes d'Egypte.
    ISBN 0-86232-806-3.   ISBN 0-86232-807-1 (pbk.)
    1. Women—Egypt—Social conditions.   2. Women's rights—Egypt.
    3. Egypt—Social life and customs.   I Title.
    HQ1793.Z4613 1988
    305.4'2'0962—dc19

Contents

Preface

This is more a personal note than a Preface. Jean Lacouture and I lived and worked as journalists in Egypt, from April 1953 to August 1956: three and a half years during which I travelled through the country and its villages in a way that was rare and privileged, even for Egyptians. This was thanks to Father Ayrout, whom I knew well and whom we meet in this book, and to the 'ladies of Father Ayrout', Christian and Jewish, who visited and helped to maintain 140 little schools where Muslim and Coptic children learned the rudiments of their language and history.

With them, and in particular with Lydia Farahat, I was able to enter those miserable homes where the poorest peasant woman would pull out from her bodice a tiny twist of paper from which she took out the precious black tea she then prepared on the 'primus'.

The years passed. Nasser introduced schools, clinics, running water, sometimes electricity. One might have imagined that habits would gradually change, especially since the women of Cairo, intellectuals, teachers, civil servants, journalists, had been fighting for more than twenty years for womens' liberation. I was stunned, on reading Wédad's study, to learn that nothing, or almost nothing, has changed, despite the laws and decrees, in almost thirty years. What! Has a revolution, and it was a genuine revolution, land reform that was supposed to liberate the peasants, compulsory education, industrialisation, the vote, the access of women to parliament and government, has all this failed to destroy the old taboos? Worse, there even seems to have been a retreat, for Muslim 'fundamentalist' women students are now going back to the old customs and to wearing the veil.

Forgive me, Wédad; I thought: 'She must be mistaken.' The

material improvement due largely to the enormous sums sent from the Gulf and other Arab countries by Egyptian migrant workers, which allow the peasants to buy a television set or a van, could not have failed to affect customs. Since 1979–1980, when your inquiry took place, things must surely have changed? And then on 23 August 1984, I read in the press that a mother had forced her sixteen-year-old daughter to commit ritual self-immolation for having been guilty of a 'mortal sin' with her cousin.

So, I feel justified in urging you to read the story that Wédad Zénié-Ziegler tells of these 'Women of Egypt'.

Simone Lacouture

'Women shall with justice have rights similar to those exercised against them, although men have a status above them. Allah is mighty and wise.'
Quran, Sura II, verse 228*

* Quoted (as all quotations from the *Quran* in this book) from the authorised translation by Dr M.M. Khatib (Macmillan Press, 1984).

Prologue

This book has its roots in my own past. I was born in Cairo, in 1940. There I lived through the collapse of Farouk's monarchy, the end of the British occupation and Nasser's revolution. Faced with Nasser, I experienced feelings of profound mistrust shared by most of the ethnic minority to which I belonged: the Greek Catholics, known as Melchites, who originally came from Lebanon and Syria.

My ancestors had left the mountains of Lebanon to settle in Egypt in the 1860s following persecution of Christians by the Druses allied with the Turks. Different peoples (Chaldeans, Amorites, Assyrians, Phoenicians) all essentially Semitic, have settled in Lebanon since 3400 BC. Of these, the Phoenicians are the most important. Industrious and enterprising, they are famous for their skill as merchants.

With the Roman occupation began (in 50 AD) the Christianisation of the country, which took place due to the preachings of the apostles, Peter and Paul. Many disputes about the dogma of the Christology arose, causing subdivisions in the Christian communities. These communities split at the time of the Eastern Schism (863 to 867) some rallying to Rome, others to Byzantium (the power which succeeded Rome in 395). Amongst them were two important communities: the Maronite which, in its entirety, chose Rome, and the Melchite, with its heavily Greek-influenced rites, which meekly followed imperial policy. Then, the Melchite community in its turn subdivided, some of its members wishing to break away from the tutelage of Byzantium to establish closer contacts with the Roman popes. Henceforth, only this branch would carry the name Melchite or Greek-Catholic, to distinguish it from the Greek Orthodox.

In Egypt, our Melchite community gradually became what is known as a *comprador* middle class, characterised by its numerous class privileges and an élitist culture instilled by French *lycées* and boarding schools, and English and German colleges. Long afterwards, I came to realise that this preoccupation with the West had cut me off from my roots and a whole dimension of my being, by devaluing Arab language and culture in my eyes.

Between us, as privileged beings, and the great mass of the people, the lack of understanding and communication was enormous. Our only links with the common people were of a hierarchical nature; every self-respecting middle-class family had in its employ one or two servants. Female staff played a particularly important role. If they were not dismissed after a few months because suspected of thefts, maids could make a career for themselves with a family. Often, they saw children born and then brought them up to adolescence, occupying a position as important as the child's own mother. Thus, very strong emotional ties linked what was called the *dada* to the various members of the family. Confidences were exchanged between mistress and servant, intimacy and affection between her and the children, but everything remained within the limits imposed by the class difference. From time to time, some member of the *dada*'s family would appear in search of charity of some kind or simply to visit their relative. They would arrive by the service entrance, and spend the entire day in the kitchen, only crossing the unstated boundary line to help with the housework.

That was how it was with Um Mohammed, the maid who brought up my brother, my sister and myself, from infancy to around thirteen or fourteen years of age. She then had to retire because she was old and sick.

We knew nothing of the home lives of Ali the cook, Um Mohammed, Messeda who succeeded her, or 'Abdu, my father's barber. A part of their lives was passed in our house. For us, the other part remained mysterious and inaccessible. We lived in different worlds. Once they had crossed our threshold they returned to the suburbs of Sayida Zainab, Mouski or Imman Al-Shafi, districts completely unknown to young bourgeois like us, and to a completely different way of life. Long after she had left, we wondered if Um Mohammed, who had been so close to us for so many years, was still alive. She had appeared a couple of times, then had completely lost touch. We owed her a great deal. It was she who, clumsily, inaugurated our sexual apprenticeship. She told us – which was more than either our parents or our school had done – how babies were conceived and born. Without mincing words, she put the matter to us bluntly and crudely without any scientific explanation to lessen the shock of such a revelation. If it was a shock for a young adolescent like me, I could imagine the traumatic effect it must have had on Um Mohammed herself, married, apparently, at nine years of age.

With the passing of time, I became consumed with curiosity as to how these shadows of my childhood had lived. For the twenty years of my existence in Egypt the absence of real contact with the common people had not concerned me, but now that I was living in Switzerland, it had become intolerable. The gulf had become even wider with my exile. Those of my social background were called by the people *khawagas* (foreigners, speaking Arabic with an accent). Despite my olive complexion and dark hair, I felt, each time I returned to my country, that I was treated as a mere tourist. That hurt me.

From my early childhood and adolescence in Egypt, so many images, long repressed obsessions began to surface. A need to clarify things in my mind became ever more pressing. I had to reconstruct this past, to confront it, in the light of my own development. I decided to go in search of the women of my country, those whom I knew, but also and particularly those whom I had passed by in ignorance and indifference. Through the testimonies recorded in this book, I have tried to retrace the course of my own existence and find the identity, the face of which I had been deprived by an alienating socialisation.

I went back in search of those who had been the shadows of my childhood, trying to penetrate their secret world, catch them in their everyday life. I went to find them in the working-class districts of Cairo and in the villages of the Nile Delta and Upper Egypt.

The poor districts of Cairo had always been mysterious, unknown to me. My only memory of them went back to the times when we drove through them in the school bus, dropping off some of my schoolmates from more modest backgrounds. None of my friends or relatives lived there. They were a 'no-man's-land' to people of my social class. Equally unknown to me were the villages I had passed through without curiosity, for twenty years, when we went on holiday to the seaside, to Alexandria, Ras Al-Bar or Suez. At long last, I discovered these places and finally saw the people living there, the men, women and children. During my investigation, I spoke to working-class women, asking them about their daily lives, the relationships within their families, their environment. I also questioned a small group of women from Cairo's intelligentsia, who told me a great deal about themselves, about the discriminatory jurisdiction that keeps women down in Islamic countries. Thanks to these interviews and my own research, I was able to put together the material that makes up this book.

Wédad Zénié-Zeigler.

PART ONE

Return to the Country of My Childhood

1
Introduction

Once again, having left behind peaceful, comfortable Switzerland, I found myself back in Cairo, swarming with its 10 million inhabitants (12 million in 1984, *Le Monde*, 30 April 1984). These last years, at each of my return visits, I had watched the city swell. The city of Cairo which, originally, was only an oasis, now stretches its tentacles everywhere. One has to remember that Egypt, apart from the narrow strip containing towns along the Nile valley and Delta, is essentially rural. Ten years ago, 80 per cent of Egyptians lived in the country; today, it is no more than 60 per cent.

In their thousands, the peasants come to congest the towns of Cairo, Alexandria, Damietta, Suez and now the newly rebuilt Ismailya. In search of an illusory prosperity, fleeing from an archaic life-style and the derisory wages available in the countryside, they swell the ranks of the Cairo's proletariat. In the overcrowded and hostile town, these country folk settle wherever they can, both in the crowded city centre and on the fringes of the residential districts. Admittedly, the Egyptian countryside, the moment one leaves behind the great urban highways and the elegant districts of the capital, is the same wherever the Nile passes through it. The irrigated fields around Giza could easily be mistaken for the cultivated areas of the Delta or Upper Egypt. Thus, for these transplanted villagers, there is no real sense of being uprooted. No place to stay? Not to worry! They will build themselves a mud house anywhere they can find a little patch of uninhabited land; in a cemetery or on a piece of waste ground. There they will contrive to cultivate an allotment which, along with a couple of goats and some poultry, allows them to feed their offspring.

In the course of my wanderings in some of the poorer districts of the capital, such as Shoubra, Sayida Zainab or around Giza, I came upon little patches of countryside in miniature. This rural emigration is not a recent phenomenon, but it has intensified since my departure. I remember that my mother did not take kindly to the arrival, many years ago, of new downstairs neighbours, wealthy villagers, who had come to take over a flat previously occupied by Greeks. These neighbours had installed in their flat, in our residential building in the centre of town, in Sabri Abu Allam Street, a veritable poultry yard. The incessant cackling of the hens and the cooing of the pigeons cooped up in the tiny courtyard adjoining the kitchen disturbed my mother who was equally upset when chickens invaded her kitchen.

Most of the women I interviewed in Cairo came from the so-called working-class districts which had been completely unknown to me in my childhood and adolescence. Finally, now, I was going to fathom the mystery, cross the barrier which had separated me from this other world. With relief mingled with shame, I entered the narrow alleys of Sayida Zainab, Mouski or Imman Al-Shafi. I was amazed to discover there the remains of that same architectural harmony seen in the engravings of Old Cairo which hung on our drawing room walls. I could imagine the lives of the women hidden behind the balcony *mashrabiyas* of the houses which seemed almost to touch across the narrow streets. Despite the poverty and lack of facilities, these districts represented to me little islands of peace and tranquillity. Outside the town, behind Saladin's Citadel, in the district of Moqattam where the domes and minarets of the City of the Dead rise up, a living population has sprung up. In the necropolises built long ago to perpetuate the pharaonic tradition shanty towns have sprung up like mushrooms. Today the City of the Dead shelters thousands of squatters from the rural areas and a population of refugees, driven out of Port Said, Ismailya and Suez in June 1967 by Israeli bombing. It is said that close to a million people live in the tombs of Cairo.

During these periods of research, my itinerary took me from the working-class districts of the towns to the villages of the *Sa'id* (the Arab name for Upper Egypt) and the Delta, depending on the opportunities which presented themselves to me. I found that, since my childhood, nothing had changed. Landscapes, customs and the rhythm of life, all seem suspended in time. Eternal date-palms stretch as far as the eye can see, cactus and wild figs cluster in tiny copses. And, along the banks of the Nile, acacias, sycamores and weeping willows bring welcome shade to the land exhausted by the burning sun. In the centre of things, the Nile, calm, majestic and immense. On the river, the feluccas pass, scarcely troubling the water's surface. Alongside the *fellahin* (peasants) and the children playing in the water, the cattle quench their thirst and soak in the muddy water of the canal. In this same water, the women do the laundry then stretch it out on the river banks. This serenity is in complete contrast to the teeming bustle of the big towns. Generally speaking, the term village can refer equally well to a simple hamlet as to a small market town, or even the principal town of an area. Whether they are in the Upper Nile valley, in Middle Egypt or in the Delta, peasant dwellings are distinguished by a certain uniformity of architecture and building material. Seen from a distance, the traditional village appears as a solid, earthy block, compact but disorganised. The houses are usually built of mud bricks which the peasant makes himself. The door to the house gives straight on to the street, hence the name *beit ardi*, meaning a house built flush with the ground. Narrow and dusty, the alleyways all look alike. Walking there when one is unfamiliar with the area is like being trapped in a labyrinth. In the scorching midday sun, the tiny village streets are silent and deserted. Stray dogs sulk on all the corners. At this time, the silence is oppressive for a 'foreigner' like me. The village has to be seen when it is alive. The villagers are early risers. The sun rises and sets very early. The peasant leaves for the fields with his cattle at dawn. Seated in front of their doorsteps, on a bench or on the ground, women and elderly men, apparently with nothing better to do, keep an eye on the children playing with sticks and stones picked up in the street. Reminiscent of biblical times, a typically semitic old man passes, sitting sidesaddle on a donkey, children running behind him. In a neighbouring thoroughfare, some peasants are selling oranges and tomatoes. A lively public market takes place twice a week on a big patch of waste land. Egyptian markets are all very spectacular: for example, the market at Al-Ghanaiyim, near Assyut in the *Sa'id*, which I have often visited.

Going to the market is almost a ritual. The preparation alone assumes a religious character. The cattle are slaughtered very early on Thursday morning and sold before the onset of the midday heat, outside the precincts of the market strictly speaking. The animal is displayed whole, the innards exposed. On the ground, traces of still fresh blood attract the famished dogs. On market day, the whole village is bubbling with excitement. It is one long procession of men, women and children, or donkeys and camels loaded with goods, marching through the streets. The actual market exhibits an enormous range of the most incongruous goods: fabrics, local crafts (especially chairs woven from palm leaves), plastic items such as shoes, sandals, bags in garish colours, cooking utensils, as well as fruit, vegetables, cheeses . . .

Crouched in small groups in front of their merchandise, men and women hawk their wares. The whole thing is a riot of colour. The women, heads wrapped in purple scarves, serve you with rapid movements, before you even have time to check the quality of the goods, the kilo of tomatoes or oranges you requested. A strange face in the village is very quickly spotted. Mine does not pass unnoticed. It is considered bad taste to bargain. After a timid attempt, I very quickly gave up when I caught the rather contemptuous looks from people, who seemed to say: 'How dare you, with all you have!'

Inside the village itself, few cars if any. One can stroll around at one's ease. In front of their houses, or in the interior courtyards, the women, in groups of two or three, make the bread. This operation, also a kind of ritual, takes place once or twice a week. The dough is made the night before. It consists of flour made from wheat, millet or dried beans, to which is added a little *helba* (cleansing cereal given to pregnant women) and shaped into round, flat loaves (about thirty centimetres in diameter). The dough is kneaded in the fresh air, on a plank of wood. Cooked in stone ovens in the houses, it gives flat, hollow brown loaves. In some regions, particularly Upper Egypt, this bread, precooked in the sun, bears the evocative name *'aysh shamsi*, 'sun bread'. It is the women of the house who, at daybreak, carry out the actual cooking of the bread which will be used all week to feed the family, neighbours or visiting friends. I have never come away from a country home without receiving two or three loaves as a gift. To this day, such bread reminds me of the taste of the snacks my mother used to prepare around ten o'clock in the morning, made of what we in Cairo called *'aysh baladi*, 'country bread', served with lemon and broad beans marinated in olive oil.

In the countryside, one of the sights which most surprises a townswoman like me is that of the churning of the cream to make butter. Ashamed of my ignorance, I did not dare ask what was inside this sort of inflated white muslin bag which, loosely attached to two pegs, looked like a suckling pig hanging on a spit. Seated on the ground, a woman was rhythmically beating with both hands the bag of cream which gradually swelled up. It is an operation calling for hours of perseverance, and is undertaken only by women. Only women, too, fetch water from the well. Sometimes, a child helps its mother pull the rope that brings up the bucket, but the woman herself carries home litres of water on her frail shoulders, toughened by the sheer weight, sometimes over a distance of several miles.

Under no circumstances can the peasant woman refuse the very heavy work required of her. However numerous, her children rarely interfere with her work. When not clinging to its mother's back, a young child will often be looked after by an elder sister (who might be only eight or nine years old), by its grandmother or another member of the family. The older children usually play in the street and do not always have someone looking after them. After school – if indeed they go – an elder brother or a cousin who has been to school helps them with their homework, something their parents, usually illiterate, cannot do. At the present moment, most villages possess at least one school. Where the state school is inadequate, private schools, built under the aegis of a religious body or some foreign or indigenous philanthropic organisation, try to offset the deficiencies. The main problem is that of recruiting teaching staff. Villages are not attractive locations for young graduates and it is usually with bad grace that a townsperson agrees to 'serve' two years in a rural district; however, this is obligatory for all graduates of state universities. Thus one may sometimes witness laxness or, on the contrary, excessive severity, and occasionally a complete lack of teaching skills, on the part of some schoolmasters. I remember going into the playground of a village school near Al-Minya and seeing a dozen pupils lined up facing the wall, awaiting harsh punishment. Another time, a group of teachers was protesting against the teaching methods of one of their staff, a twenty-five-year-old Copt, rather mystical, who insisted that the children sing religious songs before each lesson, notwithstanding the fact it was a non-religious school!

Since 1956, education has been compulsory. Despite this, thousands of children (336,000 in 1977 according to official statistics) do not attend school. It is difficult to monitor school attendance because, in many villages, literacy centres furnish lists of fictitious names in order to qualify for government subsidies. According to the Cairo press, in 1980, the number of young, school-age Egyptians working instead of attending school was estimated at 25 or 30 per cent.

In rural communities, the child can be an important addition to the workforce. Thus, parents often sacrifice their child's education to ensure the profitability of their work. Indeed, a child can help in picking cotton, herding the cows, driving the donkey and helping the *fellah* in his everyday chores.

In the village, whatever its size or importance, life is lived a great deal out of doors. This is characteristic of all the urban centres of the Mediterranean basin where the people can be found sitting or squatting on the ground in front of their houses, observing and, at the same time, part of the pageant of the street. As soon as I was spotted in the distance I was beckoned to approach. Women continually invited me into their homes to chat. The welcome is the same, whether the setting be modest or more comfortable. In the poorest homes, furniture has been reduced to the basic minimum: in a corner of the main room, a straw mattress or an old rug by way of a bed; in every home, the indispensable oven for baking the bread, the stable and the hen house. In the better-off homes, an entrance hall and spacious living-room may lead into a maze of other rooms when there is a large family. Almost all these dwellings have an interior courtyard which serves equally well as chicken-run, laundry room or kitchen (with gas ring). Because of the method of construction and the material used, these houses are cool and airy, sometimes even too cold in winter.

In the villages they go to bed early. Some homes, the most basic, have oil lamps as their only means of lighting. There is little in the way of entertainment. Television is still a luxury reserved for a minority. Among these more prosperous villagers, some also own a transistor or a cassette recorder brought back from Lebanon or the Gulf, which will be displayed with pride.

As far as administration is concerned, each village is responsible to a *markaz*, the county town of the region, which in turn is responsible to one of the Egyptian governates. The head of the village is called the *'Umda* and wields considerable power. Each village has its own structure, its unwritten laws, its customs. The latter will be more or less strictly applied depending on whether or not the village is close to a large town. Each of the more substantial villages will also have its own products and enterprises.

For example, Mansafis, a small village, has more than 8,000 inhabitants. This village, which specialises in weaving cotton rugs, is situated twelve kilometres from the town of Al Minya. The Minya area in general is highly active in cotton spinning and the textile industry, as well as manufacturing furniture.

Abu Korkas, a neighbouring village of Mansafis (approximately 15,000 inhabitants), is known as a centre for the cultivation of sugar-cane and its utilisation. Further south, in the vicinity of the town of Assyut, the village of Al-Ghanaiyim (60,000 inhabitants) is an important centre for carpentry and cabinet-making. Upper Egypt is by far the most underprivileged region of the country, while the northern part of the country, that is the towns and villages lying between the two branches of the Nile Delta and along the Mediterranean coast, is more developed.

I also spent some time in the village of Al-Serw (20,000 inhabitants), some kilometres from Damietta, a major town of the Delta. This entire region is involved in rice growing, facilitated by the plentiful supply of water.

As for the towns and resorts situated along the Mediterranean coast ('Agami, Sidi Abd Al-Rahman, Marsa Matruh), their main source of income is tourism, domestic and foreign. These holiday resorts are frequented in summer by the rich inhabitants of Cairo and Alexandria and, all year round, by the members of the numerous foreign colonies resident in Egypt.

During the 1970s, the villages (particularly those of Upper Egypt) experienced great social mobility. When they were not migrating to the major towns of their own country, the peasants were going abroad in an effort to improve their lot. I was told that in a tiny hamlet in Upper Egypt, near Girga, the entire population had moved to Rome. This is exceptional: in general, only the men emigrate, leaving their families behind. The countries of the Persian Gulf are the favourites, especially since Libya and Egypt have been in dispute. Emigration is officially encouraged by the Government, both as a way of earning foreign currency and of fighting unemployment. It is also, in many cases, the sole means, under the present economic circumstances, of guaranteeing a peasant family an adequate income or, in the case of couples contemplating marriage, of earning the money needed to start a home.

The *fellahin* of the Nile Valley, descendants of the ancient people of Pharaonic Egypt, differ physically from the Bedouins. Of Arab stock, the latter have for the most part remained nomads, migrating between the country's two largest deserts, the Arabian desert to the East and the Libyan to the West. The Bedouins can be distinguished from the *fellahin* by their finer features. The latter have coarser features. Bedouins have high cheekbones and full lips; the women are beautiful, with almond eyes, whose shape is enhanced with *kohl*, and that air of mystery imparted by wearing the *mellaya* (a voluminous black garment worn by working class women). No love is lost between Bedouins and *fellahin*; they are not prone to intermarriage. Any alliance with an outsider is frowned on in villages. Despite the resurgence, in recent years, of a latent conflict between Copts and Muslims, religions normally coexist peacefully in Egypt. An Islamic country, Egypt has, since the time of Mohammed Ali, officially shown great tolerance towards other religions, particularly towards Christianity, represented in Egypt by a whole host of rituals and cults. Present-day Copts form the majority of Egypt's Christians. It is impossible to establish their numbers in relation to the overall population. According to experts, the real figure would be around 10 per cent. Descendants of the inhabitants of Pharaonic Egypt, they worshipped Amon and Ra before being converted to Christianity by St Mark, the evangelist. Thus they can lay claim to being true Egyptians. There is an extremely large Coptic community in Upper Egypt (20 per cent of the population in the region of Al Minya alone). At first sight, nothing, either in their physical characteristics or way of life, distinguishes Copts from Muslims, other than a few external clues: Coptic villagers often have a blue cross tattooed on the palm of their hands; and the fronts of their houses are frequently decorated with pictures inspired by the bible. Certain traits such as distrust and fear seem characteristic of Copts. But the older Coptic communities in Egypt have a past, a culture and a language that is specific to them. From the point of view of customs, however, the Copts, especially in rural areas, have been strongly influenced by Islam in many ways.

No one has understood better than Jacques Berque (author of *L'Egypte, impérialisme et révolution*, 1967) both the diversity and homogeneity of the Egyptian landscape. He quotes this legend:

A Fatammid Caliph was in the habit of visiting his dominions. One day, he was passing by a village in the vicinity of Daqaliyya, too poor to detain him. But an old Coptic woman insisted on offering him hospitality. The fare, contrary to expectation, was refined. The next day, the hostess appeared, escorting a cortege of dishes, in which gold glittered. It was coins, all minted on the same date. The Caliph confessed that his own treasurer would have been unable to supply such a quantity of money minted at the same time. He asked the old woman how she had been able to amass such riches. She bent down, seized a handful of earth and showed it to him, saying: 'It comes from this.' She was right. Egypt is the gold of the soil.

2
Peasant Women of Upper Egypt and the Delta

'Women are your fields: go, then, into your fields as you please.'
Quran, Sura II, verse 223

Women of Mansafis, Al-Minya Region of Upper Egypt

My tour of villages began at Mansafis, a major village about twelve kilometres from Al-Minya, a town of some importance in Upper Egypt. I could not go wandering around alone without a base. The only place that seemed appropriate, both as regards lodging (there are no hotels or guest-houses to speak of in the villages and a woman alone would be frowned on) and to justify my presence, which might have seemed odd, was a flat occupied by a community of missionary nuns, which had been suggested by friends in Cairo. I could get board and lodging there while passing as a relative or friend visiting one of the nuns.

Starting out from Cairo, I had a train journey of more than five hours before arriving at the station in Al-Minya from which a shared taxi took me to the village of Mansafis. Like most villages in Upper Egypt, Mansafis lies some kilometres back from the main road. A canal, the Ibrahimiya, divides the village into two parts. I quickly found the flat occupied by the three nuns who made up the religious community. These three nuns (only one of whom is Egyptian) have lived and worked for some years in the very heart of the village. They have various activities: they supervise three schools built by the Association of Christian Schools in Upper Egypt, run a mobile clinic and in general try to respond as much as possible to the needs of the local population.* To this end, they organise work and spare-time activities for the village women, who are all relatively isolated. Energetic and kindly, the nuns have won the sympathy of many families who come to them with their problems, knocking at the door of the little flat they occupy above a baker's.

Interview with a group of peasant women

How many of you have been to Cairo?
Me, before I was married. Since then, never.
Why?
Because of circumstances, *el-zorouf*.
How do you imagine life in the West?
It's clean. There's lots of industry and loads of machines. Here you have to rely on your own two hands for everything.
Would you like to have electrical appliances?
We're used to working with our hands.
Which of you have been to school?

(Few hands raised . . . only two or three)

Would you like your children to go to school or stay at home?
It's up to them.
Do you have much opportunity to see each other, to get together like this evening?
No, very rarely. We're too busy.
No entertainment?
Sometimes, there's always the feast days.
Do you go to church?
Not even that.
Why don't you wear at home the modern clothes you're wearing here?
We can't. If we did people would say: 'Look at that *fellaha* (feminine of *fellah*) dressed like a townswoman.'
What people?
People in the street. *Fellahin* like us. They would laugh at us . . .
A *fellah* woman can't go about in trousers, or wear glasses.

* For almost forty years, this organisation, founded by a Jesuit father, has been involved in a programme of improvement for the villages of Upper Egypt. Around forty schools have been opened, to Christians and Muslims alike, giving a secular education, as well as religious classes for the different communities.

Must you always have your head covered?
Yes, in the street.

(Speaking to Faiza, the youngest of the group):

You're not married, are you?
No, I stay at home with my parents. I don't go to school.
Why?
I am a *fellaha*. The *fellahaat* don't go to school.
And yet some do go . . . Wouldn't you like to go?
I'm too big now. They wouldn't accept me.

(To the others):

What if she was to study at home, and do evening classes?
She hasn't got the time. She has to sweep out the house, milk the
cows, mix and knead the bread dough, take the cattle to the fields,
etc. They can't do without her in the house.

(I turn to the young girl on my left):

What age are you?
I don't know.
You don't know your age?

(Someone else answers for her):

She is fourteen.
Do you intend to get married and have children?
Faiza is embarrassed about replying. Whenever sexuality and
marriage are mentioned she blushes. She is secretly in love with the
son of a neighbouring peasant.

(To Mona, a young woman who has not spoken):

And you, how old are you?
I'm twenty.
Are you married?
For four years. I've got two children.

(To Mariam, who is about sixteen):

What about you, when will you get married?
When someone asks for me.
Is it your parents who decide on your marriage?
(Shahira, who is thirty and expresses herself very well):
Yes, with us, the *fellahin*, a girl doesn't have the right to say no to

her parents. If she does they will say: 'So, you fancy somebody else then?'

What's wrong with fancying somebody else?

It's impossible.

Is it forbidden to love?

Yes, it's forbidden to love.

There is no room for discussion. The girl must agree to accept whoever is offered to her, whether he is deformed, deaf, blind, or imbecile . . .

Since our parents have made up their minds, that's the way it is.

So you didn't choose your husbands?

No, they were chosen for us.

You didn't choose them out of love?

We love them afterwards.

So a girl in love can't marry the boy she's in love with?

It's impossible. She would be killed.

And those who become muwazzafa [a graduate, destined for the civil service]?

A *muwazzafa* is another matter. If you're educated people listen to you. If a suitor doesn't please her, people will pay attention to what she says. As for the *fellaha* nobody listens to her. She can refuse nothing and she can suggest nothing. It's not done, it's shameful.

Is it the same for Copts and Muslims?

Yes, it's the same. Our girls can't marry outsiders. They can only marry someone they are related to.

That goes for the fellahaat. What about the muwazzafin [plural of muwazzaf], is it possible for them? Does a girl who has met her fiancé at university have the right to marry him, even if he is not a relative?

Yes, it's possible.

Are you satisfied with your lot?

It's our destiny. We can't do anything about it. We've never known anything else . . .

Marsa

That same evening, I interviewed Marsa, a young Copt, about twenty years of age, who had stayed on after the group of women had left. She breast-fed her little one-year-old daughter while telling me her story.

'I have been married for two years. My husband is a peasant. At the moment he's doing his military service. He was called up when he was eighteen. He had to go to Abu Korkas, then on to the main town of our area for a medical. When he had been accepted, he was made a reserve, and he gets called up by the army whenever it needs him.

'The *fellahin* have a three-year liability to military service, whereas "educated" people have only one year. It's taken into account that the latter's families are entirely dependent on them, whereas the married *fellah* lives in an extended family, with father and mother, etc.'

I asked her about the marks on her daughter's face.

'I was holding her in my arms. I had a fight with my husband, who hit me with a stick. I tried to defend myself and the stick struck the baby who began to tremble and scream hysterically.'

During the conversation, Marsa confessed that – as I half suspected – she had not known her husband before her marriage and had not been in love with him, and she had not wanted the marriage.

'My mother is related to my mother-in-law. My mother, who is fond of money, of land, forced me to marry because my husband owned a few *feddans* of land. At first, each time she talked to me about it, I said, "no". Even my brother tried to talk her out of it: "After all, it's her that's getting married," he said. It was useless, I couldn't convince my parents. I had to give in. After putting up some resistance, I finally had to accept.

'I told myself: "It's my destiny!" Then, after the wedding, I went to live in my husband's house, with his parents. But I was much better off with my parents, before my marriage. I was more content then.

'When I was leaving my parents' house, my father-in-law wanted me to bring the sewing machine with me. My brothers said: "No, if you want her to sew, buy her a sewing machine." So he bought me one and told me: "If you want, you can do some sewing." But he had an ulterior motive; he wanted to get his hands on everything I earned from sewing! That's exactly what he did. Every time I earned fifty piastres or a pound [approximately 25p sterling in 1988] for making a dress, I had to hand it over to him.

'He supervised my every move and could do as he wished with me. He was even present when clients were having fittings. In the countryside women are very modest, you know. They were embarrassed and used to cover themselves up in front of him. He went right on looking at them and paying them compliments. He never left me alone, not even with my mother. I didn't get a chance to talk to her in peace when she came to visit me.'

Marsa's father-in-law ran a grocery shop in front of the house, a common practice in villages. Thus, he was always there, whereas Marsa's husband worked in the fields all day long. Due to this, the father-in-law with his wife's help, and doubtless the son's agreement, was able to maintain a pitiless watch over Marsa.

'My husband always thought his parents were right. Whenever I had an argument with them, he took their side and would beat me.

'There were always arguments about the money I earned as a dressmaker. Once, when I had just been paid fifty-five piastres by a customer, my mother-in-law came to talk to me and began to complain about my father-in-law who, she told me, never gave her any money, not even enough to buy herself an orange. He had taken her dowry, but given her nothing back. I felt sorry for her. After all, she is a relative! Straight away, I gave the fifty-five piastres to my husband and asked him to go and buy some oranges for his mother. When my father-in-law came in, he said to me: "Where is the money Mme X. gave you?"

'The money received from customers was always kept in the drawer of the sewing machine which stood at the foot of my bed. Having seen that there were only twenty-three piastres left, he asked me about the balance. I told him the rest had been spent on the house. He was furious and said: "Who do you think you are, spending money on the household!" I had bought some thread, a little milk and some oil. He went off to tell his wife about how I'd had the cheek to make such purchases. I was curious to hear her reaction. So I went upstairs to listen from behind their bedroom door and I heard my mother-in-law say: "Since she doesn't make enough to cover the running costs of the sewing machine and the thread, tell her to stop working." At that, I really got angry and said: "Right! I won't work anymore, if you're going to treat me like this. To hell with the machine and its owners! I'd rather clean toilets than be exploited by you!" I got dressed and told them: "That's it, I'm leaving." But, my father-in-law said: "You don't leave without giving back your jewellery."

"Whose jewellery is it, yours or mine?" I replied. To have done with it however, I took it all off and threw it at him, saying: "Now I'm going."

'But he stopped me, and sent someone to look for the priest. Being unable to find him, he had my two brothers brought over instead. They tried to bring about a reconciliation, suggesting that, to avoid any more scenes, I let my father-in-law collect the money directly from my customers. When they were alone with me, they said: "What do you expect, they're *fellahin*. They need money to plant their crops. That's why they make you work. But we can't take you away from your own home."

'In the midst of all this, my husband arrived. He began to beat me. Seeing this, my brothers took me away to my parents' house. I stayed there four days then, on my parents' advice, I went back to my husband.'

Afterwards, Marsa told me, things had been temporarily patched up until a new quarrel arose to call everything into question again.

'It was a Sunday, when we were coming back from my parents' place, where I had done some sewing. My father-in-law, having noticed it, got angry. He said: "In our house you've put the machine away; over there you've got it out again!"

'I agreed to work again, on condition that half my earnings were set aside for my daughter and myself, the other half going to them.

'Six months after this, my sister, who lives in Cairo, came to spend a few days at my parents', on the occasion of the circumcision of her three sons. I went to see her every day. We were waiting for the end of the month and the full moon before fixing the date of the ceremony. This was decided one Sunday on the way back from church. The family told me: "We've prepared everything for the celebration, the only thing lacking is new clothes for the children. Couldn't you make them for us?" So, I worked several hours non-stop to finish the three suits for the next day. An ill-disposed neighbour went and denounced me to my father-in-law. She said to him: "How hard-working your daughter-in-law is. Just imagine, she's made a profit of a hundred and fifty piastres in one day." On hearing this my husband promptly began to beat me again. Once again, I left the house and took refuge with my daughter at my parents' house. I told them my husband didn't give me a penny, neither for myself nor my daughter. Since that day, I have stayed with my parents. My husband afterwards went off to the army. I don't know if I'll have to go back and live with him when he returns. After all, I did love him after we were married. Loving your husband is a duty. Our religion demands it. I don't see any way out of my predicament. And also, I have to think of my daughter. She has to have a father. What can I do? I say to myself: "Patience, my girl, things might work out." But what if they don't? I really don't know what to do. I can't get divorced. With us Christians it's not allowed. I'm tormented by it all. What would you do in my place?'

Faced with Marsa's distress, I was very disturbed. I was incapable of putting myself in her shoes, living in a context that was too different. My first reaction might have been to advocate total emancipation to Marsa, in other words departure to a new life. But I was well aware that, for her, the only alternative was isolation, rejection by everyone, poverty and disgrace. There wasn't a shadow of a doubt: Marsa would choose the security of the family roof and the world familiar to her, however hostile. I decided that the only help I could offer Marsa was listen to what her own common sense dictated.

Um Hani

Um Hani is a young Copt woman. Twenty years of age, she was married at thirteen. She has six children, including two sets of twins; one of these has had polio. She is expecting her seventh. With the help of a voluntary school-teacher and under the auspices of the nuns who take an interest in this family, the little paralysed child, Hani, has received an artificial limb. However, in two years he has grown out of it and needs a new one; the family lacks the money. Um Hani and her family struggle under severe financial difficulties, yet they confront with serenity the prospect of a seventh child.

You said you were married at thirteen?
Yes.
And your first child, when did you find you were pregnant?
After being married seven months, I was pregnant with Hoda, my daughter. Then, a month after her birth, I was pregnant again.
Were you still breast-feeding the baby?
No, I didn't breast-feed. The doctor prescribed powdered milk for her. My kids have all been very healthy at birth; afterwards they lose weight.
You do outside work as well as running the house?
I take in sewing to help with the children's upkeep.
How much are you paid for each dress?

Not more than forty or fifty piastres. The customers bring me the fabric and I make it up.

Did you learn to sew by yourself?

Yes, if I stopped sewing we wouldn't have enough to feed the children.

Why do you have so many children if you are not in a position to look after them?

With the *fellahin* that's the way it is. We accept what comes. As for me, God has given me the strength to work for them.

So, you live entirely for your children. And your husband, do you sometimes manage to go out with him?

I never go out.

Why not, don't you want to?

It's not that I don't want to. That's just the way it is. That's how life is for the *fellahin*.

And what do you imagine life is like other than in the country?

People like you must have a nice life, restful ...

Do you ever go to the cinema?

Who would take us out? We don't even have television.

How much does a television set cost here?

From a hundred and seventy pounds to about three hundred.

Where is your husband?

In the fields. He leaves very early in the morning, carrying his tools. He comes home about three o'clock. He's tired. He eats and then rests. Later, he visits friends, brings the cattle home, then we eat and go to bed.

Does your husband help in the house?

Oh no, the *fellahin* never help their wives!

He never looks after the children?

No, the cattle need looking after, you know ... Once, I said to him: 'While I'm getting dressed, do such and such for me ...' He said: 'I can't do anything, my hands are hurting me.'

But you have a job as well!

Yes, I do all the housework ... I look after the children, I sew ... I suffer with my legs.

But what happens if you decide to stay in bed one day, because you're ill?

Never ... (laughing) if I did, straight away ...

A beating!

Yes, he would beat me. The *fellahin* are hard. They insult their wives and beat them (hearty laugh . . .), it's a fact.

And the baby you're expecting, would you prefer it was a boy or a girl?

Around here, they like boys.

Why?

With a girl, you're afraid for her . . . You're afraid for girls when they go out.

What can happen to them?

I don't know . . . They can be taken by force, have harm done to them . . .

Does that happen?

Often. There are people who are wicked, so we're afraid for our daughters' virtue. Amongst us, the *fellahin*, when a girl gets big, she doesn't go out any more. She stays in the house. After school, she goes straight home to do her homework.

Do you intend to have any more children? Do you take the pill?

I don't take the pill. I'm too weak. The doctor told me the pill was bad for me in my condition.

But your husband, he could try to do something!

What could he do? . . . (silence due to embarrassment or ignorance).

But this way you could have ten children!

Ten? (laughing). My aunt, she had twenty-four, but they didn't all live.

You are still young. Don't you want to enjoy life?

Ya salaam (ironic laugh . . .). There isn't any other life for us but this one! I almost died once.

Died?

Of weakness. I was sitting down, just like now, and suddenly I had this attack of palpitations. The doctor gave me medicine, but it didn't help much. . .

Darkness falls. Um Hani takes her leave and departs. Her tall silhouette sways along the path beside the nuns' house, wavers beneath the palm trees that stretch towards the river, then disappears.

The hamlet of Ashnin

Ashnin is a village of around 6,000 inhabitants, situated about fifteen kilometres from Mansafis on the road to Al-Minya. Its population is composed of roughly equal numbers of Copts and Muslims. As a village, it is poor and very backward. Even so, there are two schools, one state and the other private, run by the Association of Christian Schools in Upper Egypt.

As everywhere in these isolated areas, the women, curious about any passing stranger, invite me into their homes and happily agree to talk, meanwhile offering me a cup of tea, piece of bread or a few dates. I spent some time with three women: a mother and her two daughters, Aliya and Nawal, aged twenty-five and thirty respectively. My cassette recorder did not bother them, any more than it had the others. At the end of the interview, Aliya said, half seriously, half jokingly: 'Are you going to play this recording back at your place so people can laugh at us?'

Meeting with three village women

Did you go to primary school?

(Nawal replies): We went to school for only two or three years. Then we stayed at home. We don't like to go out. Our parents didn't let us go out. As soon as a suitor appeared, we got married.

Did you learn anything in the interim?

Yes, housework and looking after the cattle. Apart from that, we don't know how to do anything, neither reading nor writing. We're stuck like that, like animals.

How do you live?

We live, *al-hamdu-lillah* [by the Grace of God] according to our customs . . .

Before marrying, had you met your husbands?

Yes, we had been introduced. They had come to see us once or twice.

(To Aliya): *Do you have any children?*

Yes, I have seven children.

Do you think you'll have any more?

How do I know?

Haven't you thought of taking the pill?

No, I am too weak from housework.

(To Nawal): *What about you?*

I don't want to take the pill. I want to have children.

Why?

Childbirth is beautiful.

What do you get out of having so many children?

Those who live will pass on life to others. Those who die are in God's hands.

How can you stand death, especially the death of children?

It's God's wish.

So many children, isn't that terribly tiring for you?

Yes, we are prostrated by work. Sometimes, at night, my body trembles with tiredness.

Do your husbands help you?

Only in looking after the cattle. With us, men do nothing in the house; no cooking, no housework, nothing . . .

Wouldn't you like your husband to help a little with the cooking?

Definitely not! I just want him to leave me in peace, to stay in his place. His place isn't in the house, it's in the garage where he works.

Do you go out sometimes?

Women don't go out.

But the ones you see working in the fields? They leave their houses!

Those yes, not the others.

What about your husband?

He is old.

How old?

I've no idea. I can't even read . . . I've already told you, we're like animals.

(To Aliya): *How old are you?*

I don't know. I only know how many children I've got. (Sensing her embarrassment, the mother intervenes):

She has six children.

But how old is she?

She is thirty.

And you, how many children have you had? How many times have you been pregnant?

Many times. Seven of them died. I have four left. This one here is the oldest, and that one, the youngest.

Are they all married?

No, the two young ones are still at school.

(To Nawal): *Did you go to school?*

No, I learned nothing. I'm a *fellaha* . . .

Perhaps at that time, there weren't any schools?

There was one, but not in this village. In the main town, four or five kilometres away. Some people went to school in Al-Minya or elsewhere. But I'm just ignorant . . .That's the way it is with those who aren't very talented. I couldn't learn a thing.

And now, if you could go back to school and learn, would you do it?

No, not for ten thousand piastres.

Don't you want to be educated?

We're too old now. It's too late.

Have you been to Cairo?

No, never.

Abu Korkas

Invited by Soraya, one of the young women present at the meeting organised a few days previously, I went to visit her at her home in Abu Korkas, a neighbouring village of Mansafis.

Soraya

Soraya is thirty. She is a Copt, married to a primary school teacher (who, incidentally, was the only man present at the meeting held at the nuns' flat). Soraya has three children and lives with her family in the same house as her father-in-law, a weaver, and one of her sisters-in-law, Fawzia. Their standard of living is moderate. The story of Soraya's marriage is tied in with the arrival of her sister Alice in Upper Egypt. Soraya spoke to me about it with great simplicity and composure. Like all other women I met, she did not choose her husband. Much more serious, in her case, was her total ignorance, before her marriage, of sexual relations between husband and wife. Her wedding night was a painful and tragic experience: aware of his wife's ignorance, Soraya's husband decided to get her drunk before possessing her. He forced her to share a bottle of whisky with him, then brutally raped her (apparently he used the bottle to break the hymen). As a result, Soraya had a haemorrhage. Terrified, the husband ran from the bridal chamber shrieking: 'I've killed my wife . . .' The following is Soraya's own story.

'I was born in 1949. I got married late, at twenty-three. I had plenty of opportunities to marry but I wanted to carry on working and also I wanted a marriage that corresponded with my ideals. I didn't choose my husband. I was simply presented with him. At first, I couldn't love him because I didn't know him. We came to love each other, after the marriage. The engagement, during which I felt as if I were sleepwalking, lasted a month. I hesitated a bit, but finally put my fate in God's hands.

'Before, I had always been with nuns. That was the only life I knew. It was they who trained me in sewing and knitting.

'I worked in the knitwear factory from seven in the morning to seven in the evening and stayed with the nuns at Malawi. Then, one Saturday, I went home to my village. Sister, Alice, asked how I was. I said to her: "Frankly, Sister Alice, I'm rather upset. My younger sister, Samiha, has got engaged during my absence and the family hid the engagement from me." It hurt me a great deal to learn about it, and not to have been invited to the ceremony, since we all lived under the same roof.

'I wanted to get away from my family, to pack my bags and leave for Cairo to stay with a friend. I thought of going to live there and working with the nuns. But Sister Alice said: "Just wait, I'm going to introduce someone to you as well . . ."

'To tell the truth, I had given up thinking of marriage. I thought only of leaving. I had washed my clothes and was already packing my suitcase.

'The following Monday I was told: "There's someone wants to talk to you." It was the school teacher my sister had mentioned to me. We chatted together for a while. He asked me some questions to find out if we could get on together, then invited me to visit his family, to see how they lived. The next day I saw his sisters, the house, the furniture, the kitchen. It all inspired confidence in me. I told myself: "He must be all right . . ."

'I wanted to keep my satisfaction secret, for fear of making those around me envious. I was afraid of the village gossips. To reassure myself, I went to see Sister Alice who said: "Don't bother about what people will say. People will certainly chatter and say you got engaged to be like your sister." I went to my father and told him I didn't want the village people sticking their noses in our business. He agreed with me. Everything was clear-cut. My fiancé arrived. He asked for my hand and my father consented.

'We'll have been married six years in March. It hasn't always been easy. I had problems with my health, especially during my first pregnancy. I had to go to hospital, in Cairo. I had an operation. They tied my legs down. I lost a lot of blood. Now, since my third pregnancy, I take the pill so as not to get pregnant.

'Before my marriage, I didn't know how babies were conceived. Nor did I know what took place on the wedding night, although I had a vague idea. The day of the wedding, one of my aunts reassured me: "He won't hurt you." But nobody explained anything to me. When the time came, I fell asleep. Suddenly I woke up with a strange feeling: I was bleeding heavily.

'Afterwards, I reacted very badly. Each time my husband as much as touched me, I jumped. Later, I had my period and said to myself: "If I had known it happened in the same way as this, I wouldn't have suffered so much and nor would he." We both suffered . . .

'Some time afterwards, having pains, I went to see the doctor. He told me I was pregnant, and nine months later, I gave birth to Ines.'

Awkwardly, I ask her if she is happy like that:

'Completely, *al-hamdu-lillah*. I look after our children, the house; I make cheese. I've already filled four barrels.'

When she speaks about her husband, Soraya refers to him as Mister Adli. In his capacity as school teacher, Mister Adli is one of the most respected individuals in the village. Moreover, Soraya shows him all the more respect since he is noticeably older than her. She continues, while showing me round the house:

'This is actually Mister Adli's father's house. We live here, Mister Adli, his father, Fawzia and, at the moment, my niece, my three children and myself.

'I share a room with my three children.' (Soraya shows me a big bed that she shares with her children, while her husband and his father sleep together and Fawzia sleeps alone.)

I asked Soraya about her health and if the doctor had prepared her for the birth. I was astonished to learn that she had only the vaguest idea:

'I had problems with my health at each of the deliveries. Afterwards, things went better. Now, I take the pill. The first time I was pregnant, I didn't know what was going to happen. I had pains in the back and lower abdomen. One day, when I was alone in the house, I had violent pains, as though I were being torn apart. It was the breaking of the water. There wasn't a doctor nearby. A neighbour helped me and I gave birth then and there. Two months later, I was pregnant again, with my son. I didn't realise until very late, in the sixth month, because that time I had no symptoms. I had my first pains in the middle of the night and it dragged on for two or three days.'

I asked her how she had felt about the second pregnancy, so soon after the first.

'At first I was surprised, then shocked. Eventually, I decided to make the best of a bad job since the child was already there in my stomach and was doing me no harm. I resigned myself to it. After the birth of the second child, I took the pill for a year. After that, I had a mild nervous breakdown because I couldn't cope with things. I had to stop taking the pill because it was making me weak. Three months later, I was pregnant again. I breast-fed the baby for eight months, then I had a coil put in; but it got infected. So I started taking the pill again. That makes three years now. We'll see, after a while . . . I'll probably have another child. That would make two boys and two girls. In five years, the children will be big. I'll have my health back. It'll be over, *khalas*.'

Soraya had been a very skilled knitter. I asked if she had never thought of taking up her old profession to help her husband financially:

'Above all, I have to look after my family. I do have a sewing machine at home, and occasionally I find time to knit. Monsieur Adli wouldn't stop me. But I would only feel I had to work if our financial situation demanded it.

'With us, it's not the done thing for the woman to spend money on the household. It's the man who provides for the family and the woman must have some consideration for him. She mustn't be demanding, or ask for too many things for herself. If I want or need something, a dress or a pair of shoes, for example, I have to be sure he can afford them . . .'

Does Soraya's husband help in the house? Her reply astonished me, given the level of M. Adli's education.

'No. If he's sitting in the armchair and asks me for a glass of water, I go and get it for him. If he's hungry, I make him something to eat. I carry out all his wishes. I can't afford to be ill. Because of the children . . . Once, I was really tired. I just had to lie down for part of the day. Then my little son said to me: "Enough sleepy, mummy."

' "I'm tired."

' "If you're tired, go to the doctor." So I made the effort to get up, to get dressed and try to forget my tiredness.'

Al-Ghanaiyim (Assyut Region)

The village of Al-Ghanaiyim has recently undergone development to become the main centre of its district. It is divided into two zones: a more modern one, with good facilities, dominated by buildings, housing offices, small businesses, a bank and numerous cafés. In the other, more traditional part, live the peasants, artisans and workers, the majority of the population, which totals fifty to sixty thousand inhabitants.

Al-Ghanaiyim's geographical position means it is isolated and far from any large urban centre. It lies on the very edge of the Arabian desert. In the past, the village had a reputation as a haunt of bandits and a drug-trafficking centre. It was surrounded by walls whose gates, to make access difficult, were kept permanently closed. In 1970, the police succeeded in overthrowing the leader of the band which was spreading terror among the district's population. Since then, the village people have retained a certain mistrust and a great fear of the neighbouring mountain which had previously served as an arms depot. They almost never set foot there, except to bury their dead. The isolation of the women – more noticeable here than elsewhere – is perhaps due to this unique situation. The village has a small hospital, three doctors, one of whom has a private practice, a medical unit and several schools.

Since 1967, a community of five nuns from the congregation of Sacré-Coeur have settled in the village, just as in Mansafis. Their mission: general education, teaching the catechism to Christians, attending to public health and the general needs of the population. One of their many activities is teaching sewing to illiterate young girls, aged between fifteen and eighteen. It was under their auspices that my second stay in Upper Egypt took place, in the spring of 1979.

More sure of myself this time, I ventured alone into the main roads and side-streets of the village. One winter morning, I got up early to attend a sewing lesson, during which I was going to talk to a small group of young women. Before me walked Suad, Amal and Karima who were heading, as they did every weekday, towards the building where the sewing class took place. Their dark silhouettes climbed the dusty, deserted road. They were entirely covered by a tunic and a black veil in which a slit could just be made out. In this way one can see without being seen. This outfit is referred to locally as a *shogga*. For these three women, the sewing course is an occasion; it is their only contact with the outside world, the sole distraction in a mundane life.

Suad, Amal and Karima are eighteen, seventeen and sixteen respectively; all were baptised orthodox Copts. They are not yet married and avoid any allusion to such an event, preferring, from modesty or anxiety, not to speak of it. For them, no dreams, no hopeful waiting, no new emotions. Each has been promised, from early childhood, to her first cousin, who is no stranger to them. They grew up with him, playing together in the street. There is no parading feelings here. 'Love' is a shameful word. 'We don't say it out loud,' Suad said to me. But it is not forbidden to think secretly, and not without some emotion perhaps, about the young student from the house opposite who paces up and down on the terrace and darts furtive glances at her, while revising his lessons. Suad's destiny will be that of her sisters. The handsome Ali will have to be content to languish in silence; it is her cousin Butros that Suad must marry without protest.

Suad confessed to me that she felt bullied into it but will not revolt against the destiny her family has marked out for her. Two of her sisters are settled in Cairo, one with her husband, the other with her future parents-in-law. Suad had visited them six months previously. Although admitting that life in Cairo was much more attractive, she had returned to the village after a month, saying she had missed it. 'There's no place like home,' she told everyone who questioned her.

Suad is not completely illiterate. She failed her primary school certificate twice and was unable to sit it a third time because her mother, widowed and feeble, needed her in the house to look after her three young brothers and sisters, aged four, six and eight.

The destinies of Amal and Karima are similar. When she is questioned on the date of her marriage, Amal (seventeen), as though to postpone the eventuality, avoids talking about her fiancé Yussef, the village photographer, whom she is soon to marry. Since being in contact with the nuns of Sacré-Coeur, Karima has found a new role model and speaks of a religious vocation. She, too, has had to stay at home and give up school very young. Her mother, fragile and sickly, lost several children one after the other. Her father, a weaver, spends the whole day at his loom. They now have only Karima and another daughter, Aida, who lives at home with her two children. Aida recently lost a baby, victim of an unidentified fever, it had died on the way to hospital in the neighbouring town. Aida lost no time in conceiving another to take its place.

One evening, I took part in the following discussion with Suad, Karima, Amal and a group of their friends.

(To Suad): *How old are you?*
   About twenty.
   Did you go to school?
   Yes, I had five years of primary school. Then, Papa told me: 'It's over, you won't go any more.'
   Why?
   With us, the people of Upper Egypt, when a young girl gets big, she isn't allowed to go around alone.
   What if someone went with you?
   Impossible. My father had made up his mind.
   How many of you are there in the family?
   There are four of us: two girls and two boys. No, I'm wrong three . . .
   And did they go to school?
   No, only my brother is educated. My sister never went to school.
   What does your sister do?
   Housework, from childhood, she's done nothing but that.

(To Karima): *But don't you want to learn something?*
   I do. But it's too late. I'm dense.
   What are your housework duties?
   Sweeping, washing, making bread, cooking, doing a bit of sewing when necessary . . .
   And when it's finished, do you have any pastimes?
   Housework is never finished.
   What do you do in the evenings?
   In the evenings, we spend some time together, chat a bit, then we go to bed.
   You never go out?
   Never.
   No visiting, family get-togethers?
   Sometimes. And then of course there's also the church, you can go there if you want, in the evening. Compared to others, we consider ourselves lucky to be able to get out to come to sewing classes.

(To Amal): *Is it the same for you?*

I did six years of primary school, but I can't do anything.

But you did learn to read at school. If you had a newspaper in front of you, could you understand it?

Yes, I can read, but not very well. I read the bible a bit.

What does your father do?

He's a weaver. He makes rugs. He has his loom in the house.

(To all of them): *Which of you have been to Cairo?*

(Suad and Faiza) We have.

Did you like it? Would you like to live there?

Oh yes!

Why? What most attracts you there?

(Suad): The freedom.

What does freedom mean to you?

It's being able to go about freely in the street, in the fields, not having your every move controlled. Here, we're shut up. Whenever a girl goes out somewhere, everyone talks about it.

Is it shameful for a girl to go out?

Yes. She can hardly even go to church and, even there, she has to be wearing the *shogga*.

Do you agree with this way of life?

It's in accordance with our morals and our customs. Maybe it's wrong to live like this if you have different customs and traditions.

Do you know about customs in other towns, in other countries?

Of course we do.

Do you think things will ever change here?

We hope so. Everything changes.

Don't you think you might contribute to the change? Do you try to discuss things with your parents?

We'd like to, but nobody listens to us. They want to protect us, shelter us.

What are they afraid of?

(Furtive laughter. Suad): They're afraid of everything. They're afraid people will say: 'She went out, she came home, she did this, she did that.' It's not that they don't trust us, but they're afraid of gossip. What counts most in the village is what people will say. Can you imagine, we don't even have the right to visit a sick friend. My girl-friend, Aida, was ill. I wanted to go and see her one afternoon, but I was forbidden by my family.

Do you think marriage will give you more freedom or less?

(Karima): Obviously, a married woman can come and go as she pleases.

Really? Her husband would give her permission?

Depends on the husband. Some of them are tyrants, others are more tolerant.

So, do you hope to get married?

No, I'd like to become a nun. The sisters are a model for us, they've opened our eyes.

Could you teach sewing? If one of you decided to go elsewhere to work, as a dressmaker for instance, how would your family and friends react?

It's impossible. We wouldn't be allowed to leave, unless we had a relative to stay with. Otherwise a girl on her own can never live anywhere but her village.

Is it the same in other villages? Are the girls there shut up like you?

Throughout the Upper Egypt region, it's the same.

None of you are Muslim? Is there a difference depending on whether you are Muslim or Copt?

Apparently the Muslims have more freedom [in fact the situation is the same for Muslims] . . . It's better for them. The girls go out more often than us. We never go out.

At least there are the holiday celebrations?

Yes, Christmas, New Year and Easter for Christians.

And circumcision, is it celebrated?

Only for the boys.

Is circumcision practised on girls in your village?

Yes.

All of them?

Yes.

Did you know that in Cairo, for instance, it's not done?

Yes, apparently it's *haram* [forbidden], in Cairo.

At what age does the operation take place?

In theory at one week old, but sometimes at two months, seven months or even seven years.

(To Suad): *Were you there when your sister was circumcised?*

Of course.

Was it painful, did she cry?

Of course, she cried a lot.

But why does it have to be done if it's so painful? What is it for?
With us, the *fellahin*, it's always been done . . . I don't know why.
Did you never ask your mother?
(Suad): No, but I asked my sister. She said it was *haram* to ask. She
came to visit us that day and saw my little sister crying. She had just
undergone the operation.
Would you like to leave your village?
If that was possible, yes. But this is where our destiny is.
One day, you'll get married, have children . . .
Please, don't bring up that subject.
Why? Does marriage frighten you?
We don't want to talk about it. We can only wait.

Fawzia
Following is the interview I had with Fawzia, a young Muslim
woman who, at the age of fifteen, was married to a man of thirty-five.
She has three children, aged five, four and two.
  'It will soon be three years since the army took my husband,'
she told me. 'He comes to see me every thirty-five days and stays a
week. It's ideal. Previously, my husband was a greengrocer in
Cairo. Before, I used to live with a relative and her five children.
I don't like Cairo. I'm a real *fellaha*. I like milking the cows . . .
Look at my mother-in-law, my husband's mother. She had five
daughters, all of them are married now. Her husband lives here too.
It's nice here. Life is healthier than in Cairo. No need to go to
the baker's for bread. We bake our own. And we're utterly happy. We
go out, we go walking in the streets . . . We go out to attend the
mosque.'
  I took advantage of Fawzia's volubility to ask her some questions
on social life, health, hygiene and traditions, especially female
circumcision, a subject she tackled with much less reticence than
the other women to whom I had spoken.
  'Around here, you have a baby in hospital only if there is
something wrong. Otherwise you have it at home. I have delivered
my children alone. I love actually giving birth. Babies are lovely.
And of course, people spoil you after the birth. Neighbours come in
with bread, honey, *fetir* [a kind of thick pancake, often eaten with
cheese and honey] and all sorts of nice things. We have lots of
celebrations. Circumcision for instance. It's a big celebration. We
bring in the *tabla* [drums] and sing. It's only for boys. We give them a

zaffa [ceremony or concert]. Girls are circumcised too, but they don't get a *zaffa*.'

When I say that in Cairo girls are no longer circumcised as a matter of course, Fawzia and her companions (a few neighbours come to join in the conversation) burst out laughing, interrupted by Fawzia's indignant exclamations: 'They really don't do it? Girls stay as they are, without being cut? They don't turn out wild? Do you see this one here,' she said, indicating her daughter, 'I had her circumcised just after she was born at seven days. It's a bit painful, but it heals. It was Um Said [local midwife] who did it, with a razor. After the cutting, we put *ramad* [soothing herb] on the wound to disinfect it. When I was done, they smeared sugar on me ... [laughter from all the women there] so that my husband would like it. That's what my mother told me. I was very little, the same age as this one here (indicating a little girl of four or five). Is it really possible they don't do it in Cairo?'

Circumcision celebrations in the village

The sounds of music echo in the street. Children are playing the *tabla* and singing. The celebrations are taking place in the courtyard of one of the houses. It's the home of a young married woman, dressed in dazzling colours and decked with gaudy jewellery. One by one, several women, followed by some children, perform a belly dance. Two of them, with black skin, are from Nubia. Having arrived unexpectedly with one of the nuns from the village's religious community, I take one of the empty seats. The children surround me. I am offered a soft drink, and pressed to stay. Only women and children attend this ceremony which precedes the circumcision. The men are gathered in a neighbouring house. I take advantage of this to have a talk with some of the women present.

Which child is being circumcised?
This is one of the three.
Has it already been done?
No, not yet. Thursday, at sunset, the actual celebration begins.
Is there also a celebration when a girl is circumcised?
With girls, it's done in secret. It's shameful. It takes place without any ceremony or celebration.
Why?
That's the way it is.

I've been told it's very painful and that they really suffer. Is that why it's done in secret?

(General laughter)

Are you afraid the people nearby would be aware of what was going on?

Yes, it would be embarrassing for them.

Is the tradition still upheld here? In Cairo, there's a tendency for it to disappear?

They don't do it in Cairo any more? Here, you can't not do it.

What would happen if one didn't do it?

If it wasn't done, girls wouldn't get married.

How is it then, in Cairo, girls, even uncircumcised, get married?

It's part of our customs here. With us, in the country, a girl who isn't circumcised doesn't marry. Did you know a little girl scarcely a week old can be circumcised.

Isn't it painful for her?

No, it doesn't hurt.

Who performs the operation?

The *daya*. [midwife]

Does she have medical training?

No, but she has experience.

But when she performs the operation, is it done under proper hygienic conditions?

Yes, she's experienced. Afterwards, she can make out a certificate.

What is this certificate for?

You must have the certificate.

Why? To get married?

Yes, for the marriage, for school . . .

A girl who isn't circumcised can't go to school?

If she's not circumcised she can't marry. It's as though she was possessed by the devil . . . But, come to the party. Thursday evening, the *daya* will be there. The boys will be smeared with henna . . . And Friday morning, at seven o'clock before sunrise, the circumcision will take place.

The singing, the sound of the *tabla* and the *zagharit* [ululations to express joy by the women] interrupt the conversation.

Madiha

In Madiha's house, on a bread-baking day. Madiha lives in a big house with her four children. The three eldest go to school. Madiha breast-feeds her latest arrival while going about her work. She and the children had lived, with her husband Fakri, in a village in the Delta, Al-Waha, before coming back to Al-Ghanaiyim. Fakri still works in Al-Waha, returning from time to time to visit his family. Fakri and Madiha are in the date trade. Their house is crammed with metal crates full of dates transported from the Delta.

Do you prefer life here, or in the Delta?

It's better there. The climate is better. It's more advanced than here. The relations between men and women are better. From the health point of view, it's better organised. When one of the kids is ill, there's a doctor on hand. You're not shut up like here. Here, a woman doesn't have the right to speak to a strange man or allow him to enter into her home. He must stay outside, even if he's a relative. That's the way it is with the *fellahin*. And, in my position, I have to be especially careful about what people say, because I live alone with my children. My husband doesn't work here.

Do you think a woman has more freedom there, where you were living before?

Yes, as long as she wears the *shogga*, she can go where she likes, except in the evenings. After eight o'clock visiting is impossible; otherwise people talk.

Here, the woman is, so to speak, condemned to see only her husband and her children?

That's right.

Do you intend to have lots of children?

It's in God's hands.

What do you do during the day?

From morning till night we're busy: cooking, washing, cleaning. We tan sheepskins that we buy at the market, and afterwards I spin the wool.

Do you go yourself to the market to buy the sheepskin?

No, a tradesman does it for me.

You must be kept very busy?

Yes, and after the housework, at the weekend, I stay here to sell the dates my husband brings from the Delta. In the evenings, I'm exhausted from the day's work.

Would you like to go and live in a big town, like Cairo?

Only if my husband had work there. I follow my husband everywhere. In fact, he'll be coming back soon.

(The children come home from school, around noon, wearing coloured plastic sandals.)

Is the children's lunch ready?

Yes, they'll have freshly baked bread, and some cheese if there's any left. Sometimes, they have a meal I've prepared.

Do you sometimes eat meat?

Yes, about once a week. But there are people who can't afford to eat it at all. We keep poultry and often eat pigeon, chicken, and sometimes we have fish.

Your children have enough to eat? You live well?

More or less.

Is there poverty in the village?

Yes. The majority of the people here are poor.

(A neighbour, Fahima, comes to check if the bread they are baking jointly is ready. I ask her):

How many çhildren do you have?

I've got five and I'm expecting the sixth.

Doesn't that bother you?

I say: Dear God, give some to those who haven't got any!

In fact, you would have preferred not to have so many children?

I'm not well. I was hospitalised. When I got back from hospital, I discovered I was pregnant.

You're quite alone?

I have nobody to help me. I'm alone, with my five children. I have neither mother, mother-in-law nor sister. I have to do everything myself. I've had ten children. Five of them died. The oldest of the girls would have been twenty-two now, another seventeen, and another eight.

What did they die of?

Illness: *Hasba, nazla* [influenza; measles]. My eldest son is nineteen now. He's in the army, in Cairo.

And what does your husband do?

He's a donkey driver?

How old is he?

He's sixty-three. He was married once before and his first wife died in childbirth. Then he married me in 1956. I was seventeen. Illness has aged me a lot.

Why do you get married so young among the fellahin?

[Madiha again]: We marry young because we don't carry on at

school. At that time, women didn't get any education. Nowadays, things are changing.

Would you like your daughter to have an education?

Yes, of course.

When one of the children is ill, what do you do?

We take them to the doctor.

How much does that cost you?

Fifty piastres for a private doctor.

I was told that treatment was free in the hospitals here.

Yes, you have to get a registration form for three piastres and then go to the state hospital. If it's not serious, they treat you on the spot, otherwise you have to go into hospital.

Do most women have their babies in hospital or at home?

At home. In my case, I had the baby on a Thursday, the day we receive people to sell our dates. I was just about to make some bread. My water broke in the toilet. I said to my husband: 'It's a bit embarrassing to have the baby with visitors there. People will see me giving birth.' He said: 'God will help you . . .' I went back inside the house and, a few moments later, I brought my child into the world, on the floor. You ought to have been there with your camera!

Was it painful?

No, not at all. I took the infant on my knees, and covered her with a *gallabiya* so she wouldn't catch cold. Then, my husband arrived with the *daya* whom he'd gone to fetch in the meantime. She said to me: 'Here, let me cut the umbilical cord for you.' After she'd cut it, she put me to bed and I fell asleep.

Is the daya *always present during a delivery?*

Yes, she is called in, because you can't cut the cord by yourself.

Is it always as easy, at each birth?

Yes, this one was easy. My two other children were born as soon as I went into labour.

You felt nothing? Were you alone?

I was very tired, and I was alone. I prefer to be alone when giving birth, rather than be surrounded by my mother and the other women, except for the *daya*. . .

Do girls still get circumcised here?

Yes, I had it done for my girls.

Why?

From habit. They say you have to do it for girls, so that when they grow up . . .

Doesn't it hurt?

Yes, but it soons heals, like any wound. My youngest daughter hasn't been circumcised yet.

But you're going to do it?

Of course. Do you know that my mother had me and my sisters done when we were barely a month old. Around Cairo, it may not be done, but here it's the custom.

What's the reason for the practice?

We don't know.

Why don't you ask the village doctor about it, to understand the meaning of it?

The village doctor came here a year ago and said girls mustn't be circumcised. Apparently, it's forbidden by law [Nasser's law of 1959].

Well then, why do you do it?

We think a girl shouldn't have that 'skin'. That's the way it's always been. Each place has its traditions.

(The bread is ready . . . We notice, on the terrace of the house opposite, a woman dressed in modern clothes).

What's she doing? Is she baking bread, like you?

No, she's doing nothing. She's a *muwazzafa*. She's going to be employed by the government.

Al-Serw, Damietta Region (Delta)

'Try as you may, you cannot treat all your wives impartially. Do not set yourself altogether against any of them, leaving her, so to speak, in suspense.'
Quran Sura IV, verse 129.

Meeting with a polygamous household

In Al-Serw, a small village in the Delta, near Dammietta, I met a *ménage à trois* which, apparently, had succeeded in achieving that perfect harmony preached by the Quran. Mahmoud had married Aleya twenty-three years ago. She had given him no children. Then came Amina, some years later. No children either. Amina (forty years of age) and Aleya (thirty-five) live under the same roof, sharing the life of Mahmoud (forty-five), the carter.

A little village house, a few goats, some poultry, enough to eat and drink, a man whose favours they share, for Amina and Aleya all this seems to represent the very picture of happiness.

'We all live together. We're happy. Why shouldn't we be? We lack nothing. Each of us has her own room ... The two of us get on very well together.'

Mahmoud interrupts:

'We're organised ... I work from six in the morning till noon. Then, I come back here to get washed, in hot water ... Yes, they heat water for me ... In the meantime my room has been aired and tidied.

'The rest of the day, I spend in the market ... I hang around the cafés with my friends, that's about all. These two (indicating his wives) stay here. They don't come with me. I don't take them to town with me. That's the way it is. That's my way of looking at it. Everyone has their own way of looking at things.'

Curious to know how one could live out 'harmoniously' the situation of polygamy, I ask how other, similar households behave and if they get on as well as this one, to which Mahmoud replies:

'No, they're always fighting. They end up each keeping to themselves. But with us, there is always agreement because we have discipline.'

I asked what this discipline was and how things are organised to ensure there is no bickering or jealousy between the two women. This time, the women reply:

'Each one knows her days: seven for one, seven for the other. We were all in agreement in making this arrangement. *O'obalek.*' [We wish you the same].

I react to this wish by saying that my religion forbids it. Upon which, Aleya and Amina retort, not without a touch of malicious humour:

'Why? Tell them a man is never as happy as when he has two wives.'

Mahmoud then tells me about his job, and his daily routine:

'I'm a carter by trade. I transport corn and other goods: sand, stones, anything useful in the village. I don't own any land but I live better than those who do. I earn quite a good living. It depends on the day. Yesterday, for instance, I earned five pounds [Egyptian]; the day before, three pounds. I'm quite satisfied with that. I have enough to keep my wives, *Al-hamdu lillah!* [Thanks to God] I look after everything. I never let anyone else organise things. I go to the market, to the village. If I find meat, I buy some or I might buy some

fish or salt. I never come home empty-handed, that's the main thing
. . . I often travel alone. I'm never accompanied by either of my
wives.'

Turning to the women, I ask them if they, too, get about and if
they sometimes travel. They reply:

'Yes, we go to Damietta, Faraskur, Port Said, anywhere we want . . .
anywhere we have relatives. We always go together.'

I then ask each of the women how her day is spent. Aleya speaks
first.

'We get up in the morning, tidy and clean the house.'

Mahmoud interrupts abruptly, determined to get a word in: 'The
first thing she does, is prepare her husband's tea.'

'Yes,' continues Aleya. 'I make the tea. Then, I heat the water. We
get washed together, have breakfast together: tea and cheese, white
honey, jam . . . Then, when the man has left I go and waken this one
(indicating Amina) at eight o'clock. Then I have tea again with her.'

Mahmoud interrupts again, determined to make quite clear his
role as head of the family and *pasha*.

'She looks after my needs, then she goes back to bed until eight
o'clock . . . She has to make my tea for me. I don't even fetch myself a
glass of water . . .'

'It's like that around here,' says Amina, 'men, you have to wait
hand and foot on them.'

I verify that when it is not 'her week' one of them rests while the
other serves 'the man'. Mahmoud hastens to add: 'Yes, but if she
has to help, she does it automatically.'

I also learn that while the wives do the dishes, he goes out in the
evenings until eleven o'clock or midnight, as his fancy takes him.

'When I come home, I find each of them asleep in her own room.
Sometimes if I don't go out, we stay in together. But they never go
out in the evening,' he concludes.

Samira

Samira also lives in Al-Serw. She is from a middle-class Muslim
family of eight. When I went to see her, she was busy grilling fish,
helped by another young woman. She was happy to reply to my
questions when she had finished her work.

What do you think of the Egyptian woman?
A great deal of good. Whether she is an office worker or a *fellaha*.

And sometimes the one who is not educated is better than the one who is. She has common sense, a delicacy of feeling. Sometimes she knows more than the other. The Egyptian woman is very conciliatory. She doesn't like a lot of fuss. She is very family oriented.

But she always has to give in, make concessions! What about her rights!

She makes concessions because it suits her.

So, does the women have no rights!

What sort of rights?

Freedom for instance!

No, freedom is limited for women.

Not for the man!

With Egyptians, that's the way things are. Men have complete freedom, whereas for women, it's restricted. Men are jealous regarding their wives. For instance, if an uncle or father-in-law comes to visit him, he doesn't allow his wife to stay very long in their company. Sometimes the woman is even prevented from seeing the man who is visiting.

So, in fact, she is shut away!

In her own home. But those who can't go out don't mind, as long as the man gives them money and household expenses.

But the man does have the right to go to cafés, to go out!

Yes, as long as he brings home the money.

So, it's really all about money!

Not only money, also material well-being. You need money to be comfortable. But, for people around here, entertainment isn't very important. It's not like people in town, in Alexandria or elsewhere. I, myself, am married. And I came into a household where there were already four children. Then, I had four more and I looked after them and brought them up. Although the house is big and there's a lot of work, I'm not unhappy or bitter.

Do you have any help!

It's tiring even with help. But I'm happy to serve them and look after their comfort and well-being. And so it will be, right up to old age and death. I say this to you in all sincerity. And I thank God.

Has your husband been good to you!

Very good. Not at all domineering.

But, when it was suggested you marry him, did you agree!

No, I didn't . . . I didn't want to.

How old were you!

Nineteen. And he was forty.

And four children to look after?

Four children which he'd had with my mother's cousin, since dead. My mother took pity on these children. They couldn't be left alone!

But were you the only girl?

No, I had five sisters. All married. There was only me left. And, although I was then living in Mansurah, I was brought here to cheer up the people here. The people around here are very sorry for themselves.

3
Working-Class Urban Women: Cairo and Alexandria

'Men have authority over women because Allah has made the one superior to the other, and because they spend their wealth to maintain them.'
Quran, Sura IV, verse 34

Fatma's story

When I returned to Cairo I told my friends of my plan to look at Egypt with fresh eyes and re-experience it through the lives of women with whom I had been in contact without really knowing them. I was immediately taken in charge, shown around the clinics and family planning centres in and around the capital to see what was being done on women's behalf. But none of these visits could replace the close, direct contact I was fortunate to establish with a certain number of women of very humble background in Cairo, Alexandria and in the villages I visited. The most significant of these experiences was my encounter with Fatma, the maid of a journalist friend living in Dokki, a residential district on the Right Bank of the Nile.

During our conversations, Fatma told me about her life, her everyday routine, her dreams, her disappointments, allowing me, in my imagination, to enter into her life. I saw Fatma several times. Amused by the curiosity I displayed she would mischievously attempt to confuse me. For example, when I asked her how old she was, she first answered vaguely 'thirty or forty', then 'forty or fifty', and finally 'let's say forty' ... At times, she would try to avoid some questions, replying in a roundabout way or punctuating her statements with shrieks of laughter, as if to mock my astonishment and naivety.

A fervent follower of the *zaar* (ritual ceremony popular with the working class), Fatma had promised, knowing my interest in this ritual, to take me with her some time. I was to be informed by her or her employer of the evening when I could accompany her. For weeks I waited for her to get in touch. Insistently, I would repeat my request each time I saw her. No invitation ever came. How, in my innocence, did I ever believe that Fatma would introduce me into this secret, jealously guarded world, reserved for her and those of her social class? After all, I lived in a world to which she was not admitted!

Fatma looks like a woman of about forty-five. She has high cheekbones, dusky complexion, big dark eyes, with her hair hidden under a dark-coloured scarf. Muslim, her family originally from Nubia, she was born in Cairo and has spent her whole life there. She is her husband Ahmed's second wife. He, however, spends most of his time with his first wife, who dominates him. Fatma finds this situation intolerable and wants a divorce, but Ahmed refuses.

Fatma lives with her brother and her three children in the working-class district of Al-Hussein, near Sayida Zainab. From earliest childhood, Fatma was familiar with the K. family, because her mother worked there as a maid. The young Fatma would sometimes accompany her mother to help with her household duties, a common practice in Egypt.

Fatma's employer, Mme. K., is a refined, cultured person, from a very comfortable middle-class family. She is divorced and lives alone and has an important position on the editorial staff of an Egyptian newspaper. Fatma is almost always alone in the house; she is in charge of the cleaning and cooking. Her domain is the kitchen which serves as reception room for her chats with Nawal, the maid of the neighbours across the landing. It was there, in Mme K.'s luxurious flat in Dokki, that I went to see her several times. Squatting on the kitchen floor, Fatma, without the slightest embarrassment, replied to my questions. All the while peeling vegetables for the dinner, she spoke volubly about herself, her husband, her children, her past. This is what she told me:

'My husband is originally from a small village in Upper Egypt. I went to school for only a very short time, then I stayed at home. My mother and I brought up my niece whose mother had abandoned her. I ran the house. When I was twenty-five years of age, my mother decided I should be married. That was when I married the evil character who is my present husband.

'At that time, girls were married very young. From eleven upwards, whether they wanted to or not. That's the way it is with us. I was old when I got married. I have three children: two sons, Wahib, twelve, Khaled, six, and a daughter, Nagua, eleven. With us, women sometimes have eight to ten children, but I stopped at three. After the birth of the first, I didn't want another child, but I found myself pregnant again. I did everything to get rid of it. I banged my stomach against walls, ran up and down stairs, took boiling hot baths, had a very heavy woman press down on my hips with all her weight. In short, I tried every way to get rid of the baby. I was afraid to go to an abortionist. Lots of women have died that way. I also had an injection, but it didn't work. You know, women will try all sorts of things. Some push plants into their vaginas. For instance, some do it with *molokhya* [green vegetable used to make soup] stalks. Many of them get infected and die. So, when I saw there was nothing left but that, I gave up. My mother said: "Have the baby . . ."

'Nowadays they talk about the pill. It's sold in chemists everywhere. I tried it, but it tired me. One day, I didn't feel well, so I didn't take it any more. It was a disaster: I became pregnant for the third time. Nine months later I gave birth, at home. With us, women go to hospital only if there are complications. Personally, I don't like people around me when I am giving birth. Usually, I have easy births. I get myself ready. I get washed and dressed, I'm full of energy. When Wahib was born I had some pain because the baby wouldn't come out. So then the women around me began to pass remarks and wail, "She's going to die," they whispered. Or they said: "Here, eat something." That's why I've a horror of having people around me when I'm giving birth. When it's all over, I call the midwife to come and cut the cord. Then they bring me a meal. Each neighbour brings a dish she has prepared: some chicken and especially *helba* [cereal given to pregnant women] with honey. There's nothing like it for cleansing the system. My mother used to take it for three days. It's a sort of purge. I take it for one day, afterwards I can eat whatever I want: eggs, chicken, beans, etc. The neighbours who are there wash and dress the baby. I'm up and about very quickly and when the doctor arrives, he asks: "Where is the mother? What, you're already up and dressed?"

'Thanks to God, my children's health has never caused me any worry. I didn't want to breast-feed them, I gave them powdered milk. They are growing up and doing very well. At school they study hard and they also help me at home. But they sometimes fight among themselves. I don't want to hear another word about having children. Enough is enough. As for men, I want nothing more to do with them. I wish them all dead, they're nothing but liars. I could easily have taken my children and set up home with another man... But I am an honest woman. He'll never find another one like me.

'My husband doesn't give me any money. I have to work to provide for the children, to feed them, to send them to school. All he gives for them is four pounds [a negligible sum – a kilo of meat cost £6 to £18 Egyptian]. How do you expect that to be enough for all of us? I have to pay for their food. Yet he earns a good living. He's an ironmonger. Once a week, he comes to the house and gives each child five piastres. But it's out of the question that he sleep here. Just let him leave me in peace. I don't even feed him. From time to time, he comes to check up on my goose. I bought a fifteen pound goose which I'm fattening. We'll eat it – without him – for the celebration of Mowlid Al-Nabi, the birth of the Prophet.

'I live with my brother. He has the room upstairs, while I'm downstairs with the children. We live in a peasant style house, *beit ardi*. Now all the children go to school, even Khaled the youngest, who is six. Khaled is the best looking of the three. He looks like me. He has dark skin and negroid features, like me. Everyone here calls him Al-Numeiry. It's Al-Numeiry this, Al-Numeiry that. I'd like Nagua to be a nurse. Wahib wants to be an engineer. I tell him: "No, be a veterinarian, instead. It's well paid. Don't forget our village background." Khaled wants to be a pilot, to shoot down Israelis. He loves planes... I tell him: "You'll get yourself killed..." Their father isn't even interested in what they do. He's an idiot. Listen, the other day I was getting ready to go to school for a discussion between parents and teachers. He watches me leave and says: "Where are you off to all dressed up?" "I'm going to school to discuss your children. After all, I have to be their father as well, don't I?" He didn't even offer to go in my place.

'My mother, who helped me bring up the children, died three years ago. I come in three days a week to clean for Mme. K. and I do two days cleaning in my brother's flat. On Fridays I stay at home, and Sundays too. That's when I look after my own home, the housework, the washing. Here, at Mme K.'s I start at seven in the morning and work till two or three in the afternoon. But I have to take two buses, which means a journey of an hour and a half to get home.

'Mme K. is very nice. I'm happy with her. Sometimes she flies off the handle, but she always calms down. She pays me a pound a day. I can get by on that and I make a little extra reading coffee cups. Often, in the afternoon, people come to see me at my place so that I can read their future in the cups. Lots of my neighbours come.'

I point out to Fatma that, when all is said and done, she copes very well as a woman on her own. Her children seem to have everything they need.

'*Al-hamdu lillah*, I've got water, electricity; my children have enough to eat. It's me that's missing something. I miss a man. A man has more prestige than a woman. He inspires more respect. It's useful to have one at your side. For example, when a woman buys fruit, she'll buy one or two kilos, a man will buy four. He is embarrassed not to buy a big quantity from the greengrocer. A woman always has to bargain. Not the man. The shopkeeper respects him and doesn't try to cheat him. All we ask of a man is that he pays and assures our well-being. But I think women are worth a thousand times more than men. Life in Cairo has become very dear. It costs money to give children an education. The school itself is free. But you have to pay for all the extras: uniforms, notebooks, pencils and the rest. You have to dress children. I bought each of them a pair of shoes, some material to make up, slippers ... But, you know, the children contribute to their own upkeep.

'During the holidays, they work and earn a few pence. They work on the stalls at Khan-khalili market. So they manage to save something to buy the things they need. I put the money aside for them and buy them what they need at the holiday. I prefer to know they're doing something than to watch them hanging around in the street. In our district, people live a lot in the street. On Fridays, the children go to the cinema, at Sayida Zainab. Sometimes I say to them: "Save your money so I can take you to Alexandria in the summer." But we've never yet had the money to go.

'My husband spends most of his time with his other wife. Her, he respects; he waits on her hand and foot. The neighbours have told me a lot of bad things about her. When I heard them, I went and told my husband. He replied: "Who told you that?"

' "The children and the neighbours," I answered.

' "Bring them here," he told me.

' "No," I said. I was furious with her and with him. I'm jealous of her because she has a much better allowance than me. It's not fair. He's so afraid of her! Who knows, she could run off with another man and leave him with her children! She's got three. They're big. One of them failed his exams and doesn't go to school any more. My children have nothing to do with them. I'm afraid they'll hurt my children, hit them ... You never know ... That sort of thing happens around here. As for her, you know, she's afraid of me. She always has two or three people with her when she goes out. I walk alone. I'm not afraid of her. Whenever we pass, she gives me such a look. We say nothing, but we're always polite to each other. You know, there are some rivals who tear each other's hair out whenever they meet. Not us.

'I've chosen to stay alone. I don't want to see my husband here ... Yes, I'm fine like this. Anyway, when he does come, I fight with him and ask for a divorce. He replies: "Only if you give me a hundred Egyptian pounds." He knows perfectly well I don't have it. So, he comes here, spends the day here, stays with the children for a while; then off he goes. Personally, I have no time for him. I look after my own affairs. After all, he might at least stay with the children. When all is said and done, he acts like a guest of honour in my home. When I tell him that, he just laughs.

'I'll never get married again. There's no such thing as a good man. Men only care about loose women like mine's first wife . . .He is three years younger than me. His first wife is older than me. When he married me, she wasn't pleased. He led her to believe he was going to disown me. He'd love to come back to me. He even told me: "Give up work and I'll give you fifty piastres a day." But I want nothing to do with his fifty piastres, otherwise he'll move in here again. I don't want him; I hate him; I can't stand him. He bullied me, but he refuses the other one nothing. What's more, I've told him: "I hate you with all my heart. I can't stand having you around." So then he says, "Fine, I'll go ..." '

Meeting with Basma

'There is no way to educate a nation in which polygamy is widespread."
Sheikh Mohammed Abdu

'Agami lies on the western coast of the Delta, on the edge of the Libyan desert. The people who live on these shores and in the villages of the interior, in the heart of the desert or in an oasis, are mostly of Bedouin origin. In this arid land where once only wild figs grew, little pockets of tourism have recently appeared. Barely fifty years ago, 'Agami was merely a picturesque beauty spot, accessible only by boat from Alexandria. Today, it is a major resort for the Cairenes and Alexandrians who come to take the air on bank holidays and summer vacations. Incredibly fine white sand, a turquoise sea, a constant fresh breeze and a few, sometimes luxurious villas make up the charm of the spot.

Today, apart from the tourists and holiday makers, only a small nucleus of the indigenous population is left on the coast. The rest, having sold their land, have settled in the desert area further inland. But a small section of the remaining population, particularly building contractors, is currently reaping the benefit of the resort's expansion. The building trade has created happiness for some. These are the masons, painters, carpenters and plasterers who build the holiday homes. But 'Agami's tourist development has also created unhappiness.

Such is the fate of Basma, a young Bedouin woman of twenty-seven, whom I ran into on the beach very early one morning in April 1979.

To avoid the stares of the curious, Basma had come that morning to the secluded end of the beach to bathe, completely clothed, with her children. All the little group seemed to be wearing party clothes.

It was, in fact, the morning after a wedding. The day before had been the *shabka* [engagement celebrations] of a relative of Basma's husband. The party had gone on until three in the morning and Basma had taken part. She no longer lived in 'Agami but had recently gone to live with her mother in a village further east along the coast.

Basma's unhappiness stemmed from the second marriage of her husband, Ali, a building contractor who enjoyed a considerable reputation in the region. Not without bitterness, Basma confessed:

'Since he became rich, he has taken another wife. That's what all the men here do. The minute they have some money, they treat themselves to another woman. To console me people say: "Better to do it legally than in an illegal way." That may be true, but meanwhile, here am I, rejected and still a young woman . . . When I complain to him, he replies: "It's only natural. A man has to stay close to a new wife, at least for the first two years." '

Basma has given birth to five children, of whom only three have survived. She had been worn out by her various pregnancies (the sixth was a miscarriage), then had been diagnosed as diabetic.

A year before, Ali had married a younger woman, who recently gave him a child. Gradually, he turned away from Basma, in favour of Atteyat. Basma was hurt by this and went with her children to live with her mother at Al-Dekheyla (twenty kilometres from 'Agami). This could not last very long, since it is not in Basma's interest to keep her children away from their father. Their material well-being takes precedence over her suffering. Ali has enough money to keep both families. He even set Basma up in her own house; at least, that's what I am told by the tradesmen who work for this master builder. The elderly foreman, while chiselling away at some white stone destined to decorate the facade of a house, talks proudly of this boss, so rich he can afford two wives: 'He inherited a patch of land; he had houses built on it which he then sold. Apart from that, he owns a car and two villas, one for each of his wives, with fridge and television.'

The Muallam turns out to be an elegant young man, wearing an immaculate *gallabiya* and a *shaish* of very fine white muslin. With lordly bearing, features that are both delicate and virile, thirty at most, Ali, called the Muallam, approaches me with haughty courtesy. He wants to invite me to tea and offers to take me to the home of 'his wife'. It turns out to be the second wife, a plump little woman of twenty-two. On her husband's orders, she welcomes me with the respect reserved for foreign guests. She admits privately to me that she is not exactly thrilled to share a husband, but that she can hardly complain since Ali spends all his time with her and, furthermore, she wants for nothing. Ali, for his part, wants lots of children, as many as his wives can give him. He rules as master, gives orders that are obeyed, and does not hide his profound contempt for women.

Like Basma, thousands of other women encountered during my childhood and adolescence, had lived, and still live, with this kind of proud, silent resignation. I had only the vaguest inkling of it. Snippets of conversations, between my mother, my aunts and the neighbours, float to the surface of my memory today. They tell the tragic story of one or other of their maids, battered or abandoned by her husband.

As a child, I had no idea what suffering was involved. As an adolescent, I had my own amorous problems. Today, this reality grips me brutally, like a noise that jolts you awake after a long sleep!

Messeda

'Le Paradis est sous les talons des mères.'
Hadith

Messeda, who entered my parents' service many years after my departure for Europe, took us to her heart in the same way as Um Mohammed, the maid who had brought us up. She saw us, my brother, my sister and I, only once every two years when we went home for holidays, but my mother passed on news of us to her; she loved us as if we had spent every day by her side.

I saw her again in 1979 when I returned to Cairo to begin my research. We fell into each others' arms, moved, happy to be together again. Messeda did not really understand my work. She was even slightly suspicious, pretending to laugh, as if she attached no importance to it when I began asking her about her life. When I asked if I could go home with her to visit her family, I felt her torn between the desire to welcome me in her home and the embarrassment of seeing me turn up in a district where people of my social class never went. In the face of my insistence, she finally gave in. I ran her home in the car after work. Along the way she was full of warnings. She was particularly afraid kids would throw stones at my car unless I parked right next to her house.

Passing through a maze of crowded streets and tombs full of squatters, we reached the district of Imman Al-Shafi, next to the Citadel. This was where Messeda lived with her son, Mohammed, her daughter-in-law, Fahima and their three children. Their house was partly built by Mohammed's father on land rented from the railway company, to whom they paid £ Egyptian 2 a month. Ali, Messeda's husband, who died some years ago, had been the station master of the little local station. The railway track passes in front of the house. Beside the tracks, there are two disused carriages, and nearby a couple of railway workers have set up a tent for the night. Beyond the railway track there is only desert. In the distance rises the Citadel and, in the middle ground, Muqattam, a small hill. In the railway precinct, sixty-five families have settled. In all, 40,000 people live in the district of Imam Al-Shafi. Four or five schools have been built there. There is a hospital with twelve doctors, none of them specialised (this fact doesn't worry the people here as long as they have a paper saying they're doctors) and a birth control advice centre. The buildings of the street running alongside the railway track all look like Messeda's house: they rise straight out of the ground, of grey brick or cement, in a rudimentary style. A few goats and some pigeons walk about in front of each door; they all have their place within the houses. The entrance courtyards all have pigeon houses and an adjoining room houses the goats.

Messeda's grandchildren go to the only school in the district. Too small to accommodate all the children at one time, the school takes them in two shifts, one in the morning, one in the afternoon. My father's little car – which I have been advised to park right next to the house – is attracting the attention of neighbours and children, who are clustered around it. At Messeda's, I am received according to the rules of oriental courtesy: drinks and cakes made in my honour. It is not the done thing for employers to be received by their staff, so my visit has intrigued the neighbourhood.

Messeda is of indeterminate age; she is probably around fifty-five or sixty, but nothing in her face indicates it. Her head-scarf shows only a small part of her hair which is dyed black. A thick line of *kohl* around her eyes enhances their blackness and accentuates their laughing expression. Messeda's family is originally from the country.

Messeda was married for the first time around twelve years of age to her brother-in-law, a widower living with his daughter, Fathia. At fifteen, Messeda married for the second time – a man whose first wife, whom he intended to renounce, died soon after, leaving him a son, Mohammed. She herself has had no children. She thinks of herself as the mother of Mohammed and Fathia whom she raised as her own. As a mother, Messeda is treated with respect and consideration; this is a constant feature of the Arab family. With married sons, it is usually the mother, living as part of the household, who has precedence over the wife. Indeed, Messeda is known and referred to as Um Mohammed, in other words the mother of Mohammed. But Messeda, who is above all a woman, has been and is still exploited, firstly by her husband, Ismail, who made her run his *ta'amia* (fried, ground chick-pea) shop. Not only was she not paid for her work but she was also beaten by Ismail. To escape from the situation Messeda took a job as maid with an Israeli family living in the town centre. Well-treated, she was also sheltered – at least during the day – from her husband's brutality. In 1958, because of the political situation, this family had to leave Egypt. Messeda immediately began to look for another family. It was then she entered my parents' service. In 1979, her salary was around £12 Egyptian a month.

In the meantime, Ismail, her husband, died. His son, Mohammed, his pretty young wife and their three children, all live under the same roof with Messeda. Mohammed works for the department of health. In fact, he has two jobs which together bring in around £35 Egyptian a month. In the mornings, he works as a nurse in a state hospital and in the afternoons, as messenger for a local chemist.

Mohammed reigns as lord and master over his wife and his mother. Messeda hands over her entire salary to him at the end of every month. For some years, Messeda had spoken to us of her hopes of being able to make the pilgrimage to Mecca, thanks to the savings her son was keeping for her. A few months before the arranged date, Messeda learned that her son had had to use her savings and that the journey could not take place. Fahima, the daughter-in-law, has successfully used contraception since her third child. Mohammed, who is in the trade, brings the pill home for her. Such is not the case with their neighbour, Aziza, who is thirty-five and has eleven children, all living in two rooms. Although diabetic and worn out, Aziza refuses the pill on the grounds that it makes her unwell.

Messeda makes a point of doing her share of the housework. She devotes herself to it when she comes home from work in the afternoon and on Friday mornings, her day off. Her daughter-in-law, although friendly and respectful towards her mother-in-law, spares her none of this work. Messeda and Fahima can go out only when veiled. Mohammed strictly oversees his mother's choice of clothes and does not tolerate the slightest hint of coquetry. Bright colours and glittery jewellery are forbidden her. It took us some time, my family and I, to realise that all the presents we gave her (scarves and trinkets) were immediately filched from her to go to the grand-children.

Messeda had been sold short. Many a mother-in-law takes revenge on her daughter-in-law for her own past, as an oppressed woman. But not Messeda, who, on the contrary, bowed to the combined wishes of her son and daughter-in-law. Yet the fact of being an elderly woman ensured her a highly valued role in traditional Muslim Arab society: that of the matron, charged with the maintenance and observance of social behaviour. Messeda always stressed this point whenever she described the wedding of some relative, a niece or half cousin. Her moment of glory came each time she had to be matron of honour for a young bride. We were spared no detail of her assignment, which consisted of verifying, the morning after the wedding night, whether or not the young woman was a virgin. The nightdress or sheet stained with blood was supposed to provide the proof, failing which, the unfortunate young woman was suspected of having had pre-marital sex and thus liable to violent punishment. When such a situation presented itself, Messeda would tell us how she had preferred to keep quiet rather than denounce the young woman who would immediately have been exposed to the cruelty of an uncompromising father or brother. Sometimes, however, Messeda told us that she herself – at the husband's request – had been obliged to dilate the vagina of a young virgin because after the excision of the clitoris, the labia often contract, making normal penetration difficult.

Such practices, although they tend to be dying out in the towns, are still very widespread in the country and outlying districts. In the village, the ritual of the wedding sheet is even public. I became aware of this, two years ago, when, walking through the village of Al-Ghanaiyim in Upper Egypt, I noticed in the courtyard of a house, hanging over a line, a sheet stained with red marks slightly discoloured by the sun. I was told that the son of the house had married one of his cousins, a week before. The nuptial sheet, stained with blood, proved the young girl's virginity and upheld the honour of her husband and his family.

From time to time, after my parents had left for Canada, Messeda had gone to Sabri Abu Allam Street, where we used to live, to ask the doorkeeper for news of us. When she was told – long after it happened – of mother's death in Montreal, she sobbed and reproached my aunt Claire for not having let her know immediately.

Messeda died, in 1983, without my seeing her again. Like Um Mohammed, who raised me from birth, I shall never forget her face, her devotion, her kindness.

4
The Hidden Word

How is one to understand what all these women really mean? How to interpret their words? Reading these conversations poses a number of questions. As an urban Egyptian, an intellectual and a middle-class woman, I was obviously perceived by these peasant and working-class women – despite all their hospitality, generosity and warmth – as an outsider whom it was wiser not to trust. It took me days, sometimes weeks to allay their suspicions, to create the atmosphere of trust and complicity necessary for the truth to emerge.

Listening to the tapes and rereading my notes, I noticed certain contradictions in the stories of the women I had met. In the same conversation, for example, would appear the idea of the inferiority of the peasant woman and a great dissatisfaction at having to live out this condition along with a point-blank refusal to have the slightest thing changed. Why this apparent contradiction? I shall try to give an explanation in the following pages. Another contradiction, this time stemming from my own 'inquisatorial' approach: although I was hoping to encourage spontaneity and candour, I was aware of directing the replies of the women towards those subjects which concerned me personally, such as female circumcision, freedom to choose a husband, polygamy and contraception. I was also aware that in choosing a single topic of discussion – certain people advised me to concentrate only on the problem of family planning, others on female circumcision – my interviews would seem more like some sociological survey, and not the informal conversation I was aiming for. Thus, I chose to tackle the totality of the problems connected with the underprivileged status of women in Egypt, while remaining conscious of the risk of obtaining information that would be fragmentary, but also richer and wider. What then is revealed by the conversations that I had during my visits to Egypt?

Throughout these conversations identical themes recur, from the Cairo district of Sayida Zainab to the heart of the Egyptian countryside. Fatma, Marsa, Soraya, all the women whose voices I recorded, speak of their common destiny: that of the illiterate woman. In this respect, they represent the majority, if one remembers that 75 per cent of the Egyptian population cannot read or write. The voices of the students of Cairo University, whom we shall hear later, echo only the preoccupations of a minority. Between these two categories, the boundary is clear. It is demarcated by culture, in other words, by access to education. A great gap separates the urban world from the rural in which a much greater percentage of illiteracy is evident, especially among women. In obstinately repeating: 'We are *fellahin*', the peasant women I spoke to were stressing the limitations which their situation implies. Indeed, the expression *ya fellah* (hey, peasant!), in everday usage carries precisely this pejorative connotation. The *fellaha*, therefore, places herself at the bottom of the social ladder. She is perfectly aware of her servility and of the thankless quality of the work she accomplishes. Even the idea that she might be capable of doing something else never enters her head. She belittles herself to the extent of comparing herself with a domestic animal. Listening to these women one feels that the peasant state is the lowest of the low. To some extent it is, given the low wages the *fellah* earns. It is so too, in the eyes of urban society, which is profoundly contemptuous of the peasants and their world. Hence that form of self-contempt very common in country people, which leads to an overvaluation of education: 'Educated people get listened to, not us . . .' Without diplomas, without knowledge, one has no right to speak, these women led me to understand, full of shame at their ignorance. This shame is all the greater since they are constantly faced with the image of the success personified by the *muwazzafa*, the educated woman.

Becoming a *muwazzafa* gives access to a special status in society. The *muwazzafa* apparently enjoys numerous privileges, ranging from her choice of clothes to the possibility of refusing the husband that is offered her. She is not obliged to wear the veil. The parents no longer need to marry her off quickly since she herself will have a career and become a source of income. But, in practice, these privileges are largely cosmetic. Other than in very liberal families, the freedom to choose a husband, for instance, is still strictly limited. Only very few women gain access to education, despite the introduction of compulsory education since the revolution of 1952.

Why this impulse of rejection, so well expressed for example by the three women in Ashnin, when they claim they would not want to study 'even if someone offered them a hundred pounds'? In this paradoxical refusal of a highly sought-after education there is an element of resentment. For women of the age of Marsa, Fatma and Madiha, it is now too late to learn. They are the generation that was sacrificed. Their sole consolation is perhaps to project their secret hopes on to their children. It is in this spirit that Fatma, Mme. K.'s maid, turns to dreams. Already, she imagines her children's future and has decided on a career for each of them. Through her fantasies, Fatma is doubtless expressing the need to revenge herself for having been an illiterate child, an oppressed woman. While awaiting this revenge, Fatma, Marsa and others like them live out their destiny of uneducated women. All possibility of acquiring an education now seems closed to them. Young Karima (barely fifteen) expresses it perfectly when she says: 'My mind is blocked.' At the same time, these young women seem petrified at the slightest inclination towards progess.

In reality, these peasant women have an absolute terror of any form of evolution, of all change, of any alteration to the ancestral order; an order that is reassuring because it is familiar. Change seems dangerous to them because it implies a questioning of their entire being. An even greater peril: by not conforming to traditional rules, the disturbing risk of upsetting the social balance. To live according to the established order remains the only possible choice, even if that order is based on inequality of the sexes, economic exploitation of women, poverty, discrimination, suffering.

To return to the question of discrimination between sexes. Often, during my conversations in the villages, I heard someone say: 'Even if you already have seven boys, better to have an eighth than to have a girl.' Despite the considerable help she furnishes in doing the housework, a girl is not the precious gift represented by a boy. From the traditional standpoint, she is a burden since she must be brought up with the sole view to marrying her off. This means protecting her, shutting her up, in short, guarding her virtue. While a boy is left to his own devices and hence is free, restrictions for a girl come in many forms: from a marriageable age, a girl must remain indoors; she must not expose herself to the eyes of men. She will leave the family home only to enter that of her husband. A boy, on the other hand, needs much less supervision. Furthermore, he will not leave the family home when he marries, but will settle there with his new wife who, henceforth, will help his mother with all household tasks.

Young village women are brought up to fear the unknown. Quite naturally, they find in the family environment a shelter from the outside world. Like snails, they curl up inside their shells. The *mellaya* (also called *chogga* in certain areas) which covers them serves to maintain their anonymity, as well to protect their virtue. This garment allows them a certain protection against inquisitive looks, local gossip and slander. The 'have you heard' mentality, as we have seen, is a major factor in the provincial milieu. In their submission to social dictates, all these young women had accepted, from a very early age, that they had to give up any ideas of personal fulfilment in order to show themselves better able to fulfil the ideal role assigned them, that of wife and mother. But even having attained this rank, they are not allowed to control their own destinies. The only thing that changes for them is the authority to whom they will henceforth be answerable.

Marsa's story perfectly illustrates this attitude of unconditional obedience to parents' wishes and brothers' tyranny. Wife and mother, Marsa has nonetheless not gained autonomy. After having an unwanted marriage forced upon her, she has to await her brothers' authorisation to leave the house of a father-in-law who exploits her and a husband who mistreats her. Aware of her oppression, Marsa knows she faces an impasse. For her, there is no way out. The only escape from her painful marital experience is to return to her parents' home, for Marsa cannot divorce (for Copts divorce is strictly forbidden). What is more, she is forbidden to have any sort of relationship with another man. Leaving her husband and her in-laws therefore means for this beautiful young woman of twenty being doomed to chastity to the end of her days. Thus, as I said earlier, when Marsa, in all innocence, asked me what I would do in her place, I found myself embarrassed to find a reply. Apart from a complete break with her entire world – which Marsa cannot envisage – no solution is imaginable.

Even when they are aware of living in oppression, they have no possibility – within the closed society of the Egyptian village community – of escaping from it. Marsa, Amal, Faiza and their comrades do not have the means to flaunt the rules of their society. Docile, respectful of the established order, all these women fulfil with conviction their much-extolled role of wife. From an avid sense of duty, some of them even manage to love the husband they never wanted. The knowledge of having acted in accordance with tradition is so uplifting that their personal resentment and suffering are anaesthetised. For them, in fact, marriage is more of a submission to convention than the fulfilment of a loving relationship. In order to accept it, they have to envisage it as a sort of sublimation of the marital bond.

Soraya, when being introduced for the first time to her future husband, Adli, made an act of faith: faith in providence, faith in her own intuition. She abandoned herself to that 'long sleepwalk' represented by the period of her engagement, a period which signified mere waiting rather than romantic rapture. She prepared herself to enter marriage rather as one adopts a religion, with the firm intention of doing her best to comply with her vocation. Despite the traumatic ordeal of her wedding night, despite the suffering experienced at each of her pregnancies, Soraya has tried, in all circumstances, to live up to the very best of her character. To this end, she has made every effort, as far as possible, to practice self-denial, abnegation, respect for men, all those virtues required of a good wife and respectable mother. Without a trace of bitterness, Soraya can state that a woman must not allow herself to be ill while she is responsible for her husband and children, for the upkeep of the house and often even the cattle. With the same simplicity and a kind of painful irony, Um Hani confesses that if she goes out for a walk, she will be treated to a beating. Another story of sacrifice is that of Samira, married to a man twenty-one years older than herself, from whom she inherited three children from a previous marriage, and who gladly accepts her own tiredness for the 'well-being of her husband and children.'

I had already been struck, many years before, by this kind of resignation in some of my school friends, Copts and Muslims, from comfortable, educated families. We must have been in the first or second year of school when, suddenly, in mid-term, someone would announce to us her forthcoming marriage to a suitor who was not the 'boyfriend' we knew (from having served frequently as alibi to her parents). I had afterwards had violent discussions with my own mother, who was quite ready to accept these marriages of convenience on the grounds that 'if one has material well-being, love will follow'.

Financial security, it is true, is a far from negligible concern in all social classes, especially the most underprivileged. Thus, many women are ready to make all sorts of concessions to obtain or preserve it. Fatma, the domestic from Sayida-Zainab, would probably have accepted the presence of her co-wife if she had not found herself financially deprived. For Fatma and most of the women questioned, the man's fundamental role consists of assuring his family a basic material well-being and comfort. 'All we ask of him is to bring us in the money,' chorused Alaiya and Amina, the two wives of Mahmoud. A man who does not bring in money is unattractive, not to say useless. The man is in no way expected to help with the housework or bringing up the children. The time he spends resting and relaxing is accepted and respected. Women are there to serve him. He is there to keep them.

Social roles are well defined. A man's functions are entirely different from those of a woman, who must not put herself in his place. When Fatma has the initiative to attend a school meeting in her husband's absence, she is assuming a power to which she has no right. She is, in a way, impersonating a man in order to play a role which is not attributed to her, that of dealing with school inspectors. As such, a woman is not a valid spokesperson: she is not a whole, separate being. Like the others, Fatma has certainly internalised a sexist society's contempt for women when she expresses her shame at being a 'single woman'. The male character is haloed in an extraordinary social prestige. This prestige is probably linked with the notion of authority which, in Islamic lands, attributes to the man powers not recognised in the woman. Secure in this power, Ahmed, bigamous husband, can afford to bargain for the divorce Fatma asks of him. In fact, only he can obtain it (a woman may not demand a divorce on grounds of her husband's bigamy). Ali, the Muallam of Sidi Abd Al-Rahman, also a bigamist, enjoys an even greater prestige since he possesses a modest fortune. The power of money allows him to dole out his favours and compliments to his two spouses as he pleases. If he allows them a certain equality on the material level, he has nonetheless opted to devote himself more to his new wife than to his first. Each of them is installed in a house with her children. This is what arouses such admiration in those around him for this so generous 'boss' who is able to keep two women in style at the same time. The bitterness of Basma, a woman of twenty-seven, emotionally and sexually forsaken in favour of a younger woman, is not taken into consideration here. Admittedly, Basma is safe from financial difficulties, but, cast off and neglected, she no longer has any social standing and will henceforth experience the humiliating plight of a woman who is no longer 'useful'. The reputation for kindness and fairness which the Muallam enjoys stems entirely from his power to distribute material well-being equally. This apparent impartiality is quite misleading since, on the emotional level, one of the women has been wronged. Other situations similar to that of the trio composed of Mahmoud and his two wives, Aleya and Amina, seem to display a semblance of harmony, due mainly to the complicit alliance which is established between the two women.

Cunning is the major weapon that working-class women deploy to defend themselves against the injustice and the wretchedness of their situation. On top of this, their common sense, their realism and a certain fatalism allow them to make the best of an often harsh existence. Everything that happens or is about to happen is seen as providential, as 'God's wish'. One must therefore accept fatigue, illness, the death of one's children. From this point of view, everything appears banal: giving birth seems the most common-place event in the world. Pregnancies and births take place – other than in exceptional circumstances – without medical intervention. Only the *daya* is summoned *in extremis* to cut the umbilical cord. In working-class and rural environments, the notion of sexual modesty is extremely widespread. Generally speaking, women do not like to be examined by a male doctor. Their husbands, especially, refuse to have a male practitioner touch their wives. And women doctors are exceedingly rare in the villages and country towns. The methods employed by the local midwife are often dubious; with no medical or para-medical training, she is clearly not properly equipped; thus she will often use any means at her disposal to disinfect the uterus of a woman who has just given birth.

A doctor told me that, in their ignorance, certain *dayas* encouraged women to drink 90 degree proof alcohol after giving birth, convinced of its antiseptic effect. Throughout the recorded conversations it was the same story: practically all village women give birth at home. They undergo no medical supervision during their pregnancy. Only a woman who is afraid she is sterile will consult a gynaecologist. Sterility is a much feared defect throughout the Middle East since it is seen as sufficient pretext for a man, if he is Muslim, to renounce his wife. A similar off-hand attitude characterises the care and bringing up of children. The infant mortality rate remains quite high in rural areas, despite the creation of family planning centres almost everywhere in the country and the presence of clinics or hospitals close to many villages. The negligence of parents towards their children's illnesses is largely responsible for this state of affairs. Admittedly, in underdeveloped milieus, the slightest illness not treated in time in the case of a child whose resistance is weak, can be fatal.

The very structure of the village or urban working-class district – in fact, a quasi-replica of the village – imposes a communal way of life. Everyone has a hand in bringing up the children; mutual aid is very common, provided people are on neighbourly terms. Social events are the responsibility of the entire population. Births, marriages and bereavements are everyone's business. Fatma described – not without irritation – the invasion of her relatives and neighbours, come to make a fuss over her new-born baby and take charge of it. Each event is celebrated in spectacular manner. Male circumcision is celebrated with a certain pomp. Not so female circumcision, which preferably takes place behind closed doors. Funeral rites and bereavement receptions also have an important social function. At Al-Ghanaiyim, I attended the funeral reception of the husband of a young woman of twenty, married for three years. The young widow's modest home had been taken over by the entire local female population. A neighbour had also placed her house at their disposal, to allow the many women who had gathered to use it for the reception. In a house at the other end of the village, male mourners were being received. For three days, the cortège of women came and went. Squatting on the ground around the widow, they improvised laments in praise of the deceased. In the kitchen, a few women busied themselves making bread and little cakes for the guests. After these festivities, the young widow had to lock herself away for months on end to live through her sorrow and reminisce about the departed with anyone who visited her.

Another ceremony called *zaar* was frequently referred to by

Fatma, the domestic from Sayida Zainab. It is, in fact, a favourite meeting-place for women. The *zaar* is a traditional ceremony designed to chase off evil spirits, the *affrits* which haunt the imaginations of Muslims and Copts and manifest themselves in the form of possessions and exorcisms. One has only to come in contact with these spirits, after an illness or violent grief, for them to take you over or haunt you. The *zaar* is a very common ceremony, especially among the working class. As such, it serves women as an escape from their confinement, representing a place where they can unburden themselves of their miseries and the dramas of everyday life (illness, sterility and any other suffering).

Superstitions, rituals and religious events hold a predominant place in the lives of women from the country and working-class districts of the towns. They are the cohesive element of the social group. Each individual participates fully in them. When Marsa makes the clothes for her nephews' circumcision celebration, she is fulfilling a social function. It is the same for Fatma who, isolated from her social group, would have no real life. But she draws her strength and radiance from the dubious fame she has acquired within the community. Fatma fulfils an apparently innocuous role which nonetheless has its own importance in a society where superstition is widespread: she reads fortunes in coffee cups. As such, she is a very popular figure. The local people come to consult her. She holds a certain power over their destinies. In the same way, Messeda, a woman bullied all her life by her husband, gains her self-esteem from her role as local matron: safeguarding the virtue of young women is a heavy responsibility when one remembers all the taboos surrounding virginity in Muslim Arab society. As women, Messeda, Fatma and Marsa have no real existence of their own. Only the social roles they fulfil within society guarantee them the possibility of being recognised by others and of maintaining some sort of dignity and self-esteem. This is tantamount to saying that these women, whose difficult lives I have partially evoked, find a sort of well-being in this harmony with the existing social order (the word *mabsoutin* – literally, 'we are content, satisfied' recurred frequently in these dialogues). This view of things no doubt corresponds to a certain reality. It lacks one essential element, however. Fatma, Um Hani, Messeda and thousands of others like them do not yet realise (even though they feel it vaguely) that their submission to the existing order radically hinders their own personal growth.

Through rituals, beliefs, social prejudices, the words of these women reveal their subservience to the world of tradition. Their words also underline the major problem in contemporary Egyptian society, that of family planning. Throughout my interviews with these working-class and village women, we have witnessed the recurrence, like some leitmotif, of the impossibility for most of them to practise contraception in any sustained way. None of the reasons put forward by them are truly convincing. What they reveal above all, is an unacknowledged fear of contraception. Islam does not officially oppose it, despite the extreme position adopted by certain religious dignitaries. Fertility, however, is a basic value and the *Quran* exalts the role of wife and, even more, that of mother. It must not be forgotten that in rural society, the child represents an important financial aid through its participation in the work of the fields. One must also take into account the fact that country people marry very young and that, consequently, the rate of reproduction is increased.

What is being done in Egypt to solve this problem? 'A child is born every twenty seconds!' This is the alarm sounded by means of publicity posters to try and combat the scourge of overpopulation that afflicts Egypt. In 1983, Egypt's population was estimated at 45 million. At the time of Nasser's death, in 1970, it was calculated at 34 million and, according to forecasts, by the year 2000 it will be 65 million. Yet a vast family planning programme was set up as early as 1965. An organisation called the Supreme Council for Population and Family Planning was created for this purpose. This organisation set out to increase the number of advice centres, the first eight having been opened in 1955. Faced with the immensity of the task, the Council, at the instigation of the head of state, established a ten-year plan with the agreement and participation of the Ministries of Education, Health, Religious and Social Affairs, as well as the Arab Socialist Union, the sole political party. The aim of this plan was to reduce the birth rate by 1985 from 34 to 24 and the rate of mortality, especially infant mortality, from 14 to 11 per thousand. The means employed to achieve these goals consisted of a public information campaign through the mass media, as well as the creation of centres which put at women's disposal up-to-date contraceptive methods. By 1978, there were already 2,500 public centres of this type and 437 private social services. In rural districts, these centres are called 'Health Units'; all sell the pill at the nominal price of five piastres. Some of the centres, in the poorer districts of the towns, attract a substantial clientele. On the other hand, I have sometimes seen completely deserted Health Units in the villages I was visiting.

Amongst the private, but government-subsidised, family planning centres, one has to mention the large social centre at Boulak (a working-class Cairo suburb), directed by an extremely dynamic woman, Mme. E. Tabet, of Swiss origin. This centre, which, among other things, runs literacy classes for young people and directs the agricultural activities of the district, is equipped with an obstetric and gynaecological clinic as well as a modern laboratory. As for Cairo's Family Planning Association, a private organisation encouraged by the Ministry of Social Affairs, it is extremely active both in Cairo itself and the villages of the Delta. Its woman director, Aziza Hussein, tackles the problem of contraception from a different point of view from that of the official services. Mme. Hussain and her team try to encourage people to share in solving the problem. By integrating contraception into a more comprehensive community programme, the Family Planning Association of Cairo hopes to involve not only women, but also, and especially, men. The problem of contraception is also being tackled within the framework of the training given to children's nurses, for example, as well as through other activities relevant to women and children. It was in 1963 that Aziza Hussein initiated this technique, with the help of a small group of Egyptian women (Cairo Women's Club) in a village in the Nile Delta, Sandyun (thirty kilometres from Cairo). This pilot project gave interesting results and encouraged the association to follow it up, paying particular attention to the education and training of small groups who, working on their own, could go on to involve the local populations.

Enormous sums have been invested at government level to solve the problem of limiting births. Foreign aid plays a large part in this. Various research programmes and projects have been undertaken by UNICEF, the Ford Foundation and many other organisations. The American Development Aid Agency (AID) has donated $25 million to Egypt to finance a birth control project; American volunteers have even taken charge of certain local centres. That of

Sayida Zainab, in Cairo, has benefited from such assistance, but despite impressive efforts, the family planning campaign has not achieved its objective. On the contrary, the birth rate has considerably increased. What is more, although abortion is illegal in Egypt, a report from the World Health Organisation gives figures of 150,000 to 180,000 illicit abortions in Egypt.

To what is this failure to be attributed? Surveys recently undertaken show that only a tiny proportion of women were affected by the campaign. Those able to read and write are more easily convinced than the illiterate. Raising the consciousness of the latter is slower; very often they attend the family planning centres at around thirty-five years of age, after having had at least three children. As we shall see later, the underprivileged status that women endure in the Arab world is the major stumbling block towards the recognition of the need for a serious family planning programme. As long as woman's lot remains unimproved, the fear of being deserted or of finding another woman acting as one's 'stand-in' will persist. Most women of humble background believe they can best hold their husband by having as many children as possible, in order to compete with their rivals. Thus, fertility remains a gilt-edged security, especially for those women who are financially dependent on their husbands. One has also to contend with the glorification of fecundity as the supreme proof of male virility. An ancient attitude unlikely to disappear.

5
The Modern Woman

The veiled students of Cairo University

Childhood friends, Egyptian women who had remained in Egypt after my departure, offered to accompany me to the university to meet students. The *hejab* (Islamic dress) worn by an ever-increasing number of students, going by the name of *mohajibaat*, particularly interested me. It was thus that I entered, for the first time, the precincts of Cairo University, located at Giza on the road to the Pyramids. The university is a beautiful structure inherited from the monarchy, divided into various buildings. Classes are mixed, yet in the classrooms the *mohajibaat* refuse to sit beside the boys or to have the slightest contact with them outside.

These students, with whom I talked at length, voiced a scathing criticism of the laxity of the moral standards of Western women; they themselves maintain an extremely conventional attitude towards men. The conversations I had with two groups of women, one unveiled, the other wearing the Islamic veil, are reproduced below.

I spoke first to the unveiled women.

What do you think of the present-day Egyptian woman?
Life isn't easy for her.
Are you representative of the majority of Egyptian women?
No, we're a minority.
Do you consider yourselves to be liberated women?
Yes, compared to others.
Do women have the same rights as men?
Yes, in the public sphere but not in the private sphere. There, they are underprivileged in many respects, compared to men.

But, since civil rights do apply to women, can't they take advantage of them to improve their situation, to make themselves heard?

In that respect the situation has improved. It is now possible for women to lodge complaints and make demands, but the law hasn't followed suit. It hasn't caught up with the changing situation.

Do you consider it reasonable that a man has the right to divorce and not a woman?

No, it's unfair. The man can even renounce his wife without her knowledge.

And there's no way to protest?

The law is like that. It comes from the religion. It's the application of Islamic *Shari'a* law.

Can nothing be done to change or relax the law?

No, nothing.

Do you think woman is inferior to man? Is that why the law favours men?

Yes, indeed, women are much more impulsive than men. That's why they are not given the right to divorce without the husband's consent. If they had the right, they would invoke it for every little quarrel. Men, on the other hand, are more thoughtful, more in control of their actions.

And yet, in the marriage contract, there is a clause allowing the woman to ask for a divorce on the same grounds as the man?

Yes, the *Isma*. But it's optional. No self-respecting woman with any consideration for her future husband would dream of asking for it. Very few women take advantage of this right.

Why?

So as not to upset her future husband. He might feel he was being dominated by his wife. In any case, to enter a marriage anticipating divorce from the word go, is very much disapproved . . .

By whom?

By the family, by society . . .

Don't you think that some precaution is necessary to avoid finding yourself tied for life to a man you can't stand anymore?

Maybe, but one dare not take it.

So, you're not entirely free?

Of course we're not free.

How can you accept such a situation?

I don't. As a woman, I feel uncomfortable.

So, what's the answer, in your opinion?

It's up to the woman to do what is necessary to keep her husband. If he leaves her to look elsewhere, it may well be her fault. She has to try to understand why he didn't stay with her.

What does one have to do to hold on to a husband?

That depends on each individual woman. Each one has to discover how to hold on to her husband.

How can a woman control her husband's comings and goings?

The woman has to choose the man she's marrying and trust him.

Does the woman always choose the man she marries?

No, not always. But nowadays, in the towns, there is much greater freedom of choice. It varies from family to family. In mine, for example, it's out of the question for a girl to name the boy she wants to marry. He has to be introduced to her. In any case, it's forbidden to associate with men before marriage.

You can't go out with a boy?

It's possible in a group, but never alone.

But if you're interested in one of the boys in the group?

His intentions must be serious.

In that case, could you see him alone?

It depends on the family. Some are less strict than others. But, if you want to observe Islamic law strictly, a man has only to hear the voice of a woman who is not from his family for it to be sacrilege, like seeing her face or hands . . .

Are many of the women students married?

Yes.

(Of the fifteen students present, six are married.)

Do girls still get married when very young?

No, not any more, because they go to university or have jobs . . . Also, there is the great problem of accommodation. There aren't enough flats available for young couples.

Do girls go to university while waiting to marry?

Yes, but they do it out of necessity. Nowadays, a young man asking for a girl's hand wants to know what diplomas she has before asking about her family's financial situation.

So, your daughters can look forward to a different kind of life. They will have careers much earlier. This will achieve autonomy much quicker. How are you preparing them for this? Are you instilling in them the same standards that you were given?

It depends whether you're modern or traditionalist. We believe in giving them a little more freedom, but with certain limitations.

Such as?

For instance, we disapprove of the behaviour of Western women. They have abused their liberty. It's gone beyond the limits of decency. Here we could never accept such permissiveness. We would never accept the sight of women walking about on beaches with bare breasts, pornographic films, or allowing young people to have sexual relations outside marriage. The West really has no shame. Everything is disappearing. Our own society still respects certain values. We maintain our standards, our respect for the law and conventions, for our religion.

In short, the Western woman is not the ideal model for you. You don't at all envy her 'liberation'. What would your ideal woman be?

Perhaps a synthesis of occidental and oriental.

What do you get from your university education?

A broadening of outlook, a chance to develop your personality and to understand life better.

Is that important for the advancement of women?

Yes, an educated woman has a particular place in society. What's more, she no longer dominated by circumstances. She dominates them.

In real terms, what form does that take in everyday life? Do you manage to assert yourself at home, with your husband?

The man is always the master.

When you go out, do you feel you have a contribution to make? Can you take part in men's conversations?

In general, at middle-class social functions, the women chat on one side and the men on the other.

What do you get from your university training with regard to bringing up children?

An educated mother is better than an ignorant one.

Do you take part in the political life of the country?

No, very few women take any interest in politics.

Even in university circles?

Even there.

Is there a women's liberation movement at university?

No.

You told me earlier that you weren't altogether free, that there was still inequality between men and women. Don't you think that is reason enough to rebel?

We've been brought up this way.
Don't you ever question that upbringing?
It's difficult. There are acquired habits you can't shake off easily.
But in time, things will change.

I then spoke to the group wearing the Islamic veil:

Why are you wearing the veil?
Our religion insists on it. According to Islam, a woman must
allow only her hands and the top part of her face to be seen by
others.
*Women stopped wearing the veil in 1932, thanks to Huda
Shaarawi. Why turn back the clock, sixty years after such a victory?*
Before colonisation, women dressed like this. It was the Europeans
who imposed their way of dressing on us. We want to go back to the
very source of Islam, to rediscover our identity. Our movement is a
revival of Islam.
Is it a sort of protest against modernity?
No, not necessarily. But we want to obey the precepts of Islam to
the letter, in order to please God. It is God who commanded us to
dress this way.
*Isn't it a sign of women being effaced again, after so much effort
expended to bring them out of their seclusion and propel them
towards public life?*
On the contrary, we would like to serve as models for all women
nowadays.
Do many of you wear the veil?
Thousands.
Do you have special principles, rules of conduct?
No, we abide by the rules of modesty.
What do you think of the position of the Egyptian woman?
It's the most progressive of all women's.
Do you think she has the same rights as a man?
A distinction has to be made between things that concern
women and those that concern men.
Do you consider yourselves to be liberated women?
Yes, in a way.
What is a liberated woman?
A woman who does what she wants.
Everything?
Yes, bearing in mind the norms of our society.

Then freedom has limits. What are they?

With us, for instance, it's forbidden to go out alone, either openly or secretly.

For a single woman or a married one?

It's the same for both. We may not speak to a man in the street.

But, here at university, you sit on the same benches as male students and you have male lecturers!

Yes, we can talk to them, but only within the university precincts.

But what if you run into a student or one of your lecturers in the street?

We pretend not to know them.

Do you feel excluded by the other students, or do they accept you easily?

We are integrated with the other students.

In the street, don't you sometimes come up against nasty remarks from passers-by?

Sometimes, someone will call us *Sitt Al-Sheikha* or just make fun of us. But we don't care. God is with us!

Modernity and fundamentalism

The young women who attend university put forward an argument that is progressive, organised and coherent. But in their everyday lives, from both the emotional and the domestic point of view, they suffer from the same oppressive forces, the same contradictions as do the illiterate working-class and village women. Today, Egyptian women students are living out a unique drama: that of the confrontation between religious fundamentalist ideology and Western inspired modernist ideology.

In Egypt, modernism is represented by a minority comprising the indigenous middle class of Turkish, Coptic or Syrio-Lebanese origin as well as the new class of *nouveaux riches* which emerged after Nasser's revolution and became particularly visible after Sadat's introduction of his open door, the *infitah*. This new social class, composed mainly of army officers, tradesmen and business men has opted for the Western model, a trend which inevitably intensified with the appearance on the Egyptian market of consumer goods and luxury items imported from abroad. The last ten years have witnessed an ostentatious display of fashionable clothes and the latest gadgets made in France, Britain or the United States, Hong Kong or Germany. These goods are a constant provocation to those who cannot afford them. The imbalance between the standard of living of the privileged minority and that of the majority grows every day.

Since the democratisation of education, universities are attended both by young people from these backgrounds and those from more modest backgrounds from the villages or the urban working-class districts. The women from less well-off backgrounds who nowadays go to university have taken a step beyond their peasant sisters, but, for the most part, they still confront material obstacles stemming from their financial circumstances. Going to university or being a working wife and mother remains problematic for them. They have to face the practical problems of all sorts which arise in towns: child-care, looking after the house if they have no help at home, distances to travel, to mention only a few. So, being an active professional, far from representing a chance to bloom and develop, means more servitude for women; which amounts to saying that learning is 'élitist'. Such a statement may seem paradoxical since education has been democratised since 1956. One has to appreciate that for those who do not come from a privileged class, financial and material circumstances are a serious handicap in present-day Egypt.

Listening to these young women, one has the impression that the greatest resistance to change comes from themselves. They do not question a system which they nonetheless find unsatisfactory and oppressive. They exhibit the same inertia observed in the village women, inspired by a fear of any change. In the towns, this attitude is all the more intense since women are directly confronted with the signs of this threatening modernity. They have a certain awareness of the danger inherent in change, whereas peasant women have only a vague presentiment. Hence this refusal of 'Westernisation' and the retreat into traditional values. From there to accepting regression, is only a step! To combat the internalised insecurity, the psychological instability whose threat they vaguely perceive, these young women readily avail themselves of old clichés, such as: 'The man is always master', or: 'It's up to the woman to do what's necessary to keep her husband . . .' They criticise the Western model, which is both enviable and unattainable: 'Western women have no shame . . .' And, more and more, they take shelter in religious rigorism.

Thus, a phenomenon is making its appearance in the big towns: the return to the *hejab*, the Islamic veil. This phenomenon, which is not confined to Egypt, is due to the tide of fundamentalism that has swept through all progressive Arab countries (Syria, Algeria, Tunisia and, particularly, Iraq and Iran). This veil, or shawl, is worn in different ways. Many of these veiled women could be mistaken for Catholic nuns. They wear a white headband which, covering the hairline, allows only the oval of the face to appear, before dropping to form a sort of breastplate covering the shoulders and chest. It is worn over a long dress of a dark or drab colour (usually grey or blue). Other women are currently wearing a white crotcheted head-dress, that covers them down to the neck, worn over any long skirt or dress. The most austere women, usually younger, dress entirely in black. The face is hidden behind a cloth mask with two small slits for eyes. They are wearing the *Nikab*, the outfit worn by the wives of the Prophet Mohammed, in the eighth century.

What is the origin of the veil? Here is what the *Quran* says in the Sura of Light (Sura 31, verse 24), on the need for modesty imposed on women:

Enjoin believing women to turn their eyes away from temptation and to preserve their chastity; to cover their adornments (except such as are normally displayed); to draw their veils over their bosoms and not to reveal their finery except to their husbands, their fathers, their husband's fathers, their sons, their step-sons, their brothers, their brothers' sons, their sisters' sons, their women-servants and their slave-girls; male attendants lacking in natural vigour, and children who have no carnal knowledge of women. And let them not stamp their feet in walking so as to reveal their hidden trinkets.

At the beginning of the Islamic era, the veil was a symbol of social prestige in Egypt. Made of precious materials, it was worn mainly by wealthy women. The women of the people, who could not afford such luxury, adopted a substitute, the *mellaya*, which they wear to this day. The obligation to wear the Islamic veil was officially abolished in 1932. The feminist movement, which had sprung up in the wake of the nationalism of the years 1919–20, placed the suppression of the veil at the head of the demands concerning women's emancipation. Paradoxically, nowadays, the return to the veil is being called for in a similar spirit of resistance to neo-colonialism that has re-established itself in Egypt.

In present-day Egypt, the women who decide to wear the veil are, as we have seen, mainly students, not only from Al-Azhar but also from Cairo's three other universities and those in the provinces. One meets them in the vicinity of these establishments and in the centre of the capital, walking in groups of two or three, rarely alone. In general, they elicit a certain respect from passers-by, but also the occasional sarcastic witticism. In any case, they do not go unnoticed in the midst of the great sartorial carnival that strolls the streets of this town.

Indeed, the pageant of Cairo's streets is fascinating, picturesque and endlessly instructive. There, you meet a medley of young bourgeois dressed in the latest Paris or London styles, *fellahin* wearing the eternal *gallabiya* and hippy tourists in outrageous outfits. This motley population daily rubs shoulders in a country where most workers earn between fifty piastres and a pound a day and where a tiny minority of the upper middle class often squander fifty to a hundred pounds in an evening.

It is impossible to guess the social class of a veiled woman. The *hejab* is a refuge. In other words, it is, for the most part, a means of disguising poverty, of overcoming shame. Other motives, some explicit, some unacknowledged, prompt Egyptian women to wear the veil. When one questions a veiled woman, she will often invoke religion: 'We are calling for a return to the authentic Islam.' She will then refer to the famous Quranic *Sura* quoted earlier and to the sayings and deeds of the Prophet's life (the *Sunna*). But it remains to be seen whether, behind this form of protest against the goverment's inegalitarian, pro-Western policies, the fundamentalists will reveal authentic religious convictions.

Religion in Egypt throughout history, has been a gilt-edged security, a sort of rampart behind which men have withdrawn in ages of unrest. To combat alienation, Westernisation and the frustrations and inequalities brought about by neo-colonialism, Muslim Fundamentalism proposes a global solution: a return to the sources of Islam. In other words, a return to a pure, egalitarian, spiritual community of believers, based on the model of society founded by Mohammed.

Behind the generic term Muslim Brothers, fundamentalists are in fact divided into various, often rival tendencies all sharing the same ideal. The most fanatical of these is the movement *Al Takfir w'al*

Hijra. This group did not shrink from using violence to demonstrate openly its hostility to President Sadat's policies. It is thought to be behind most of the outrages which have taken place in recent years, some in universities, others aimed at the Coptic Church, and indirectly responsible, through its influence on young army officers, for the assassination of President Sadat in October 1981. If, however, the majority of veiled women currently call themselves the Sisters of Mohammed, it does not necessarily mean they belong to any of these semi-clandestine fundamentalist tendencies. And one might reply to the question raised earlier by suggesting that it is not the most fanatical political extremists who hold the strongest religious convictions.

Let us look again at the remarks made by the group of veiled students from Cairo University, in Giza. In the matter of their private lives, these *mohajibaat* pride themselves on their rigorous and austere moral code, while, at the same time, claiming to be free. Their sphere of freedom is extremely limited, since it excludes all contact with men, other than their husbands and immediate male kin. The inconsistencies and contradictions of their statements apart, what immediately stands out is their anxiety to find a solution, other than traditional subservience or the aping of Western trends. It is not a simple business. The process is like that of a people which, after being liberated from colonialism, searches for its own identity. The rejection of the oppressor's culture, even if it seems like regression, may well be a necessary stage in this search for a national identity.

Alibi-women

The history of Egyptian women is, however, more than just a long, reluctant submission to tradition, to religion, in short: to the power of men. Certain women, at the cost of superhuman efforts and countless risks, rebel and try to create their own lives. First and foremost, there is the small, but socially influential group of Egyptian women, almost entirely emancipated, self-aware, creating their own desires, free. One cannot say enough about the growing influence exercised by women within the Egyptian intelligentsia. There are journalists, film-makers, actresses, diplomats and even ministers. Amongst all those I met, I shall mention the names of Samiha Ayoub, director of the Egyptian National Theatre, Inji

Aflatoun, well-known artist and militant, Latifa Al-Zaiyat, also a militant nationalist from the 1946–52 period, Inji Roshdi, feminist and editor of the daily paper *Al-Ahram*, Mirvat Al-Tallawi, diplomat attached to the Ministry of Foreign Affairs, Farida Naqash, writer, Layla Inan, lecturer at Cairo University and Layla Abu Seif, film-maker.

All these women are engaged in a professional or political activity on the same grounds as men. Their success is all the more praiseworthy in that it takes place on difficult terrain: that of a 'phallocratic' society, very much disinclined to give up its prerogatives. Some of these women spoke to me about their struggles, the difficulties and obstacles they have encountered. Emancipated and free, these women are still very often perceived as prototypes of a 'masculine' woman who inspires in men the fear of being dominated, of losing their prestige and, hence, their virility. What is more, they serve as alibis for those who claim that women enjoy the same advantages as men. But the price paid for this emancipation is high. Very often, these women are forced – to safeguard their freedom – to make painful, agonising decisions: for example, renouncing marriage and a family in order to establish a new identity.

The emotional, intellectual and social ravages experienced by these women pursuing prestigious careers is, however, as nothing compared to the problems facing a girl of humble background who decides to defy social condemnation. The story of Hind, the young girl from the provinces who, to escape from a marriage arranged by her family, decides to flee the country and, entirely alone, go abroad, exemplifies an entire generation of rebel women.

Hind, the story of a runaway

At twenty-three years of age, Hind left the village of Talla, near Al-Minya, in Upper Egypt. Five years later, she arrived in Switzerland where she still lives. I met her in the office where I worked as a welfare officer, when she was pregnant. For two years, I accompanied her in her various undertakings and tried to give her all the help she needed.

Hind is the youngest child of a middle-class Coptic family. Her father being dead, Hind lived with her mother and sisters, under the domineering protection of her elder brothers. Having finished school, Hind had begun her second year of business studies at

Al-Minya University. Gifted and intelligent, she was destined for a career in the Egyptian civil service once she had obtained her diploma. She would then have enjoyed the status of *muwazzafa*. Yet Hind was not content with her lot. She was free only up to a point. In the sphere of her private life, she was entirely dependent on the goodwill of her brothers and her mother. They had decided to marry Hind to a relative she did not love. She resisted the project and made scenes, to such an extent that her family claimed she was mentally ill and threatened to have her committed to hospital. Through university channels, Hind arranged to go to Germany on a summer course and managed to escape from her family. When the course was finished, she contacted a family living in Switzerland who agreed to take her on as an *au pair*.

Things started to go wrong when the P. family, after a few days trial, decided not to keep her, for reasons that are not clear. Overnight, Hind found herself kicked out of the P.'s house, denounced to the police as being in the country illegally (she had come with only a tourist visa), reduced to leading a parasitical existence in an unfamiliar town where she barely spoke a word of the language. Caught red-handed stealing from a grocer's, she is kept under surveillance by the police. The Home Office delays its decision: will Hind be sent back to Germany or repatriated to Egypt? While her future is being decided, she is placed with the Salvation Army, her personal belongings and passport taken from her.

Overcome by panic at the thought that she might be repatriated on the first plane, Hind, abandoning passport and suitcases, decides to flee. She hitch-hikes a lift to Geneva. Friends in Egypt had given her the name of a fellow Egyptian working for the United Nations, but she is unable to get in touch with him. After several days wandering the streets, leading a dangerous, precarious existence, she meets a young Swiss, the manager of a bar in the town centre. He takes pity on her and offers her a place for the night. Robert is Swiss lower middle class. He has little education and, at twenty-five, lacks any specific professional qualification. His world is that of discotheques and bars. He has not travelled and barely knows where Egypt is on the map. His idea of the Arab world is limited to a master–slave relationship between men and women. For Robert, Hind is a dream come true. At last, he has someone to dominate. Hind's stay is extended. She soon allows herself to be seduced. From time to time, she gives a hand in the bar without pay. After two months, she discovers she is pregnant and that, according to a family planning centre, it is too late to terminate the pregnancy. She still has no work, no resident's permit. More than ever, returning home is out of the question.

Robert's family, self-righteous Protestants, pressurise him to marry Hind; he is not in love with her. He is reluctant to 'tie himself down', but he does not want to appear as a 'swine' either. So he proposes marriage to Hind. Afterwards, this decision is constantly put off due to the couple's frequent changes of heart. Robert gradually turns out to be brutal and possessive, all the while displaying a contempt for Hind that is tinged with racism. Hind also proves to be jealous and demanding. She asks Robert to treat her like a European and not to regard her as an 'oriental slave'.

At little André's birth, his parents still have taken no decision regarding their plans to marry. Robert legally recognises his child who will therefore take his father's name and nationality; but this does not solve Hind's problems. Even though she has given birth to a Swiss child, she is still legally a foreigner as long as she remains unmarried to the child's father.

Hind may have a taste for emancipation, but there is no way she can see herself bringing up a child on her own. Returning to her family in Egypt would be suicidal. Not only is Hind not strong enough to withstand society's condemnation, but more importantly, she runs the risk of having her son taken from her and put into an orphanage for ever. The only solution is marriage. For that, she would have to 'knuckle under', agree to be docile and submit to Robert's desires, wait up till he comes home every night, at one or two in the morning, let herself be raped when he is drunk. Undecided, Hind drags herself from one welfare office to the next, looking for help in her search for work. Working temporarily in a shoe shop, she is underpaid because she is working illegally. On top of this, her health is causing problems. She cannot look after little André and work at the same time. So, Robert's parents look after him. Finally, the couple marry, only to divorce shortly afterwards. What is happening to her at the moment? From the point of view of marriage and family life, it is a fiasco: fragile, Hind is unable to wage war on two fronts. Her parents-in-law have taken complete charge of her son's upbringing. Hind continues to struggle along to achieve autonomy and dignity.

After having listened, having tried to understand what has emerged from the stories and conversations of these women from town and village, one fact has become clear to me: for the Egyptian woman, living in a Muslim or Coptic environment, the laws and customs sanction the total supremacy and arbitrary power of man.

PART TWO

The Chains of Law and Custom

6
Sexual Rites

'On that day the dwellers of Paradise shall think of nothing but their bliss. Together with their wives, they shall recline in shady groves upon soft couches. They shall have fruits and all that they desire.'
Quran, Sura XXXVI, verse 55–56.

Introduction

In Muslim Arab society, everything connected with sexuality is subject to taboos. Yet no religion has so lyrically glorified romantic passion, sensuality and the joys of physical contact: no culture is so permeated with eroticism as the Islamic. Arab literature abounds in treatises and manuals which are like hymns to the beauty of woman and the pleasures of sex. The famous *Thousand and One Nights* is one of the monuments of this literature. Its erotic vision unites the very essence of the *Quran* and the sacred texts of Islam in which the spiritual and the sensual are indissociable. Here is Abd Al-Wahab Boudiba (*La sexualité en Islam*, OUF, 1975)

> Islam is an ethic founded on life and lyricism, on the legitimacy of satisfying desire and the complementarity of man and woman ... Love is a work of God. It is therefore the symbol of the perfection of Allah's creation. God is glorified as the donor of pleasure and the instigator of all joy. God is perceived as a pillar of love and an abiding incitement of Eros. For the orgasm is a marvel which helps us to be aware of the efficiency of God. To have an orgasm is to become worthy to read in the book of creation.

Throughout the preparation of this book and during my conversations with the women of Cairo, Alexandria and the villages of Upper Egypt and the Delta, I collected a mass of invaluable information on the sexual restrictions that oppress women in this society. A women's body and sexual responses – capable of so much sensual gratification – are, from earliest childhood, subject to the laws of society. The latter encourages and sanctifies sexual union strictly within the limits of marriage. Outside this, it is utterly forbidden. Numerous rituals accompany the various stages of a woman's life, rituals designed to guarantee that her behaviour be consistent with the 'values' extolled by society.

In the name of these same 'values', little girls, women in their thousands, in Egypt and elsewhere, undergo brutal attacks on their physical and spiritual being; whether it be circumcision to protect the virtue of pubescent girls or the defloration carried out by an older woman on a young bride to facilitate the husband's vaginal penetration. As for prostitutes, they suffer imprisonment or stoning. Unmarried mothers, considered to be criminals, are often put to death by their own families

Female circumcision

When the subject of female circumcision – so very taboo – arose in my interviews, it aroused reactions of embarrassment and reserve if not astonishment or mockery at my own curiosity and indignation. Although they may not deny the painful aspect of the operation they are forced to undergo, there is a definite tendency on the part of these women to make light of the suffering and to stress the beneficial end result. Every woman – especially the poorest – has had to learn to bear pain, to overcome it! Furthermore, the idea that this operation could in any way represent a 'mutilation' does not even enter their heads. To their eyes, circumcision is a necessary step towards a woman's sexual maturity. It is a sort of 'rite of passage' that leads her straight to marriage.

By means of evasive answers, veiled explanations and embarrassed laughter, I was made to understand that, in a traditional society, a woman has no right to sexual desires or feelings. All that is expected of her is to be ready to endure, coldly and chastely, her husband's onslaughts. The most effective method of preserving a girl's chastity and of guaranteeing her fidelity after marriage, is purely and simply to amputate the organ capable of procuring her any erotic pleasure. Removing the clitoris, an organ unnecessary for fertilisation, also means reducing woman to her primary function: motherhood.

This seems perfectly logical for these women since, living in a society that is sexually segregationist, they have completely accepted the division of roles according to sex. Since the beginning of time, it has been agreed that the joys and pleasures of sex are reserved for men, and the dignity of childbirth and motherhood for women.

Since it is entirely in keeping with traditional values, there are no grounds for Fatma, Fawzia or Suad to question this infringement of their rights which leads to so many others. Thus, they will take pains to perpetuate the practice, as long as they have failed to understand that such sacrifice is pointless and is part of an immense 'plot' designed to put them at the mercy of male domination.

The practice of female circumcision, which remained unknown for many years (apart from a few specialists, ethnologists and sociologists) has recently been revealed to the general public, thanks to the active intervention of humanitarian movements, such as 'Terre des Hommes' and various Western feminist movements. International opinion has only recently become involved. Conferences dealing with the subject have been organised, notably by the World Health Organisation (WHO) at Khartoum in February 1979 and at Alexandria, in collaboration with UNICEF, in March of the same year.

These conferences were followed up by a massive press campaign. Certain magazines took advantage of the situation to publish articles and photos that were more in keeping with horror films, designed to arouse reactions of outrage and cast discredit on the 'barbaric' peoples implicated in such practices. This adverse publicity was resented by the inhabitants of the countries in question since it cast aspersions not only on a sexual practice, but also on a cultural world which represented security to them. One can understand them. African women's organisations reacted violently to this intrusion from outside. Today, the debate continues and is intensifying.

First of all, it is necessary to give a clinical definition of female circumcision, and its implications for the health and welfare of women. Technically speaking, female circumcision, or excision is the removal, more or less complete, of the external female genitalia. There are three main forms of excision. The 'mildest' and by far the least practised, going under the name of *Sunna*, consists of the removal of the prepuce or the tip of the clitoris (sometimes both) by means of a sharp instrument (usually a razor blade). The form that is most widespread throughout Africa, excision properly speaking (also known as clitoridectomy) consists of the removal of part or all of the clitoris and and the labia minora. Often, the interior lining of the labia majora is also cut away. Any sharp instrument may be used to carry out these operations. This ranges from a kitchen knife to a razor blade, by way of the pointed winding pin of a primus stove, a reed stalk, a nail, or even a piece of glass.

The third form, the most brutal as well as the most drastic, is infibulation (from the latin *fibual* meaning hook or clasp). Apparently it was practised by the Romans to prevent fornication amongst their slaves. It is also called 'pharaonic circumcision' by the Sudanese and 'Sudanese circumcision' by Egyptians. It consists of the removal of the entire clitoris, the labia minora and most of the labia majora. When the operation is over, the two sides of the vulva are then stitched up, but the vaginal orifice is reduced to the minimum (the diameter of a pencil), allowing just enough space for the passage of urine or menstrual blood. Here again, all sorts of techniques are employed (stitching with thorns, cauterising by firebrand) to close the labia majora which then swell up, then sewing up with thread with the aim of guaranteeing the almost total occlusion of the vulva until the wedding night. At which time, the husband will undertake to open it. Afterwards, it will be enlarged each time the woman gives birth and then sewn up again. Frequently, the occlusion is such that the husband (as we have already seen) has to call the 'matron' before being able to penetrate his wife. An important point: there is no similarity between circumcision, a prophylactic measure recommended for boys in almost all societies, and excision whose main aim is to diminish, if not completely repress, the sexual desire of women.

One cannot excuse or condemn the practice of excision without trying to understand the ideology that underpins it. Certain authors have tried to ascribe to excision a religious, particularly Islamic origin, despite the fact that it is practiced in many non-Islamic societies, including Christian. Research has shown that it goes back much further than Islam. It already existed, apparently, at the time of the Pharaohs. A Greek papyrus, dating from 162 BC mentions it clearly. It is still impossible to say whether this practice originated with an ancient African puberty rite which spread to Egypt or if it is a relic of Pharaonic times or indeed a mixture of both. What is clear, is that it is not mentioned in any Quranic instructions; only a single *hadith* refers to it. This is a phrase the Prophet Mohammed is reputed to have addressed to Um Attiya, whose job it was to carry out excisions, when he said: 'Reduce, but do not destroy.' Indeed, it is on the basis of this *hadith* and on its interpretation by Islamic scholars that sunna excision is justified in Egypt.

In Islam, excision is invested with a quality of 'purity' (indeed the literal translation of the Arabic word for excision, *tahara*, is 'purification'). We know that bodily cleanliness is one of the most rigorously observed precepts of the Muslim religion.

A number of myths surround excision. In some societies a hermaphroditic nature, common to man and woman, is considered to exist, in other words, the belief in the presence in one sex of a characteristic of the other sex. In women this presence is thought to take the form of the clitoris, hence the need to remove it. Disencumbered of this virilising appendage – the clitoris – the woman can now assume her true feminine nature and the capacity to bear children. This myth is echoed in the Pharaonic belief in the bisexual nature of the gods which, by extension, would also be seen as a human attribute. The essential male and female essences are localised in the respective genital organs of the man and the woman. In order to integrate men and women in society, each of the sexes must be able to eliminate that part of the other which it contains. It is only by undergoing excision that a girl becomes a complete, separate woman and is then ripe for marriage.

Strengthened by these convictions, about forty countries in Africa and the Arab world have for centuries submitted their young girls to this mutilating practice. Apart from the African and Middle Eastern countries in question, the practice of excision has been noted, to a lesser extent, among certain peoples in Upper Amazonia, Australia and Northern Peru.

A few statistics will give an idea of the scale: in Mali, 95 per cent of the women of Bamako (ethnic group Bambara) have undergone excision; in Egypt, 75 per cent have undergone it (whether it be total or partial removal of the clitoris); in Somalia, 98 per cent of women undergo excision or infibulation.

It must be added, particularly in the case of countries such as Egypt, that these practices tend to be dying out in urban environments, except among the poorer classes or those with rural backgrounds where traditional values linger on.

Of these practices, only sunna circumcision, a comparatively mild operation, has relatively few after effects. The other forms of excision all have serious consequences from both an organic and a psychological point of view. Performed without anaesthetics, they can become traumatic events for a little girl. Here is the account that Aisha, an Egyptian woman of twenty-six, gave of her excision, performed when she was eight years old.

'My mother had told me the week before. I was very happy; I thought it would be fun. The day before, I had my hands and feet dyed with henna. I put on a white *gallabiya* covered in embroidery. It was like a party. The next morning, the local midwife arrived with another woman. They told me to lie on the floor. They twisted my arms so that I couldn't move and pinned my legs to the ground after pulling them wide apart. The midwife rubbed a little alcohol on my genitals, then she cut me with a razor. My mother, my aunts, the neighbours, they were all there. I screamed with pain. I was given a glass of lemonade and put to bed. Then they rolled the pieces of flesh that had been cut off in salt, wrapped them in cloth and tied it on to my arm. I kept it on me like that for a week, to protect me from evil.'

Even more serious are the medical consequences resulting from rudimentary hygienic conditions and inadequate disinfection of the wound. Haemorrhages and infections of all sorts arise from these factors. A doctor from a small village in Upper Egypt told me of several deaths from tetanus following excisions performed under unhygienic conditions. This does not include complications of an obstetric nature. Many Western obstetricians dealing with circumcised patients report that they have to resort to Caesarean operations.

In the practice of excision, the midwife is not the only one who may be involved. A survey was carried out in 1979 in Egypt by Marie Assad, a lecturer at the American University in Cairo. It involved fifty-four women, clients of a family planning centre in a working-class suburb of Cairo and reveals amongst other things that: 54 per cent of excisions were carried out by the *daya* (local midwife); 16 per cent by fortune-tellers; 13 per cent by barbers; 12 per cent by doctors; 6 per cent by nurses.

The most serious consequences for women's health are those resulting from pharaonic circumcision or infibulation, which is often responsible for serious gynaecological or genito-urinary complications (the formation of cysts, abscesses, stones, injuries to the bladder, rectum or the urethra). In Sudan, 20 per cent to 25 per cent of all cases of sterility have been attributed to this type of circumcision, which often causes an irreparable frigidity. According to Dr Gerard Zwang, excision permanently anaesthetizes the clitoris; this basic erogenous zone has been reduced to a mere area of scar tissue, the woman is deprived of all possibility of orgasm.

Conscious of the malpractices and abuses caused by excision, some countries have tried to introduce legislation aimed at limiting or banning it. Somalia and Sudan have declared it illegal although it is precisely in these two countries that it is most widespread. There has, however, been official encouragement to replace pharaonic circumcision with sunna. The late president of Kenya, Jomo Kenyatta, reintroduced female circumcision in 1962 after decolonisation. In 1959, Egypt, by a decree of the Ministry of Public Health, banned 'unauthorised' excision, in other words, when not practised by the medical profession, and advocated *Sunna* circumcision rather than the clitoridectomy (the form most widely practised). This decree forbids the *daya* to perform surgical operations of any kind, in order to avoid the complications caused by lack of hygiene which are responsible for most infections. Futile prohibition, for village women are generally very reluctant to be treated by doctors and surrender themselves with much more trust into the inexpert hands of the local midwife. So far, no law opposing female circumcision has really been operative. The power of conformity and custom remains even stronger than the fear of penalisation.

Under the circumstances, the fight against female circumcision must first of all exert influence on women's consciousness. Indeed, no law, decree or ban will be effective until those most concerned, the women themselves, become conscious of the harm done to them and the alienation they experience. Reading the numerous accounts given by women who have undergone excision, one is amazed by how many of them, despite the suffering and shock they have endured, plead in favour of maintaining the practice, advancing reasons of a moral or medical nature or, in the case of

Muslims, of fidelity to the tradition of the Prophet Mohammed.

It remains to be seen to whom the task of convincing women will fall. That is the subject of the great debate currently preoccupying African women's organisations, Western feminists, ethnologists, humanitarian organisations and international agencies. As we have seen earlier, some African women's organisations have given little encouragement to the anti-excision campaign conducted by Europeans whom the problem does not concern. Thus, at the Copenhagen Forum convened by non-governmental organisations in July 1980, on the theme of 'Health', a delegation of women from West Africa headed by two women ministers (one of whom was Jeanne Martin-Cisse, of Guinea) walked out of the meeting in protest against this kind of campaign and against the presence of a European woman presiding over the Forum.

It is true that the European's women's attitude was one of ethnocentricity, revealing a total absence of comprehension of the cultures and customs of the peoples concerned. They should have looked more deeply and sensitively into the matter and taken into consideration the opinions of those most concerned. The trauma of colonialism has not yet been effaced and one can understand that peoples who have been oppressed are reluctant to accept lessons coming from those who dominated them for so long.

In defence of female circumcision, ethnologists and other scholars have advanced the need to respect the cultural 'authenticity' of others, whereas humanitarian organisations and international aid agencies have been trying to decide who ought to alert the appropriate authorities. As far as the culture of others goes, I am less inclined to respect it when, in fact, it encourages practices which lead to oppression and suffering. As a woman, I cannot remain indifferent to anything that hinders the growth and development of other women. Thus, I believe that female circumcision must be opposed at all costs: because it denotes contempt for and discrimination against women by men, because it prevents women from fully experiencing their sexuality and because it is a violation of their physical wholeness. Practised on defenceless children, it can be experienced as traumatic and involves serious risks to their health and future.

That organisations charged with health and welfare and other research institutes organise conferences on female circumcision to which they invite representatives of the countries affected by it, seems to me a first step. These conventions have made it possible to make the governments in question aware of the need to rethink the problem in the light of the changing status of women. Certain of these governments have shown themselves ready to take measures at school level, aimed at creating a better health education. At the same time, there is an attempt to improve the training given to medical and para-medical staff. Amongst other things is envisaged the 'reorientation' of local midwives, so as not to devalue their social function in the villages.

Laws and decrees banning female circumcision are – as we have already seen – quite futile as long as men will not give way on the matter, and as long as women themselves have not understood that it is completely justifiable to demand their dignity and freedom. Women's organisations in Africa and the Arab world, certain religious groups and even some government authorities are slowly coming to understand this and to tackle the problem. But means – particularly financial – are lacking in most of these countries. A few non-statutory organisations in Europe and the United States have already started to finance projects relating to the distribution of educational material (books, audio-visuals, etc), or to training (courses in sex education in schools, training for children's nurses and midwives, retraining of village midwives) aimed at explaining to children and adults just what female circumcision is and why it must be combated.

In the light of such considerations, a working party on female circumcision was created in Geneva in 1978,[1] attached to the United Nations Sub-Committee on Human Rights. Its aim is to collate all material relating to the subject (gathered from conferences and meetings on the theme of health) and to encourage the governments of the countries in question to initiate programmes aimed at raising awareness in their populations, by giving encouragement and financial support to projects currently being undertaken by various non-statutory organisations. This group is in contact with several women's organisations in Africa and the Arab world, as well as government authorities concerned with health issues. To monitor progress, its African woman president has already made several field trips and established contact with those in charge of the projects. It is to be hoped that these operations which, as yet, are being carried out at the level of small rural communities affecting only a few regions of Africa, will gradually extend to all regions where excision is practised.

Defloration: the obsession with virginity

Defloration is frequently carried out, generally when the husband encounters resistence from the hymen, when it becomes necessary to facilitate matters for him. In the villages, the *daya* undertakes this operation. With scant consideration, sometimes even quite roughly, she inserts her finger into the vagina of the young woman to pierce the hymen.

An Egyptian woman doctor, Nawal Al-Saadawi, a gynaecologist and psychiatrist, relates in *The Hidden Face of Eve* (Zed Press, 1982) that, in the course of her career as a gynaecologist, she had to spend countless nights attending young women bleeding to death after the piercing of their hymen by the *daya*. Indeed, it sometimes happens that the latter, applying a little too much force, reaches the uterus and sometimes even the bladder, causing lesions of these organs. The victims of such practices are powerless and ill-equipped to resist this invasion of their bodies. What is more, they have actually given their consent, failing which they would become social outcasts.

In traditional Muslim Arab society, the fetish for virginity is very constricting. The idea of sexual liberty for women, of self-determination regarding their own bodies, is still unacceptable. A woman's entire education, and the social guidelines laid down for her, derive from this obsession with virginity, and its preservation is strictly supervised by society. The slightest indiscretion is severely reprimanded. This surveillance is most stringent in villages and among the urban working class where the influence of tradition is much stronger than in Western-influenced milieus. It is brothers and male relatives who have the right and duty to 'punish' a guilty woman, and this can take the most horrifying forms (strangulation, drowning, poisoning). The justice of the family clan is pitiless. The slightest suspicion (without even waiting for proof) is liable to incur death. Accounts of atrocities committed in the name of honour abound in literature and in news columns of Arab countries.

One news report, some years ago, told how a young Egyptian engineer, upon returning home after some time studying in Germany, found a bottle of medicine in his sister's possession which he was told was an abortifacient. He immediately put the girl to death. The autopsy on the victim revealed that she was not even pregnant; a simple delay in the onset of her period had apparently terrified the poor girl who had secretly gone to the nearest chemist to find a 'cure'. At the trial, the lawyer representing the brother-executioner pleaded the motive of family honour, and the judge acquitted the murderer.

Very often, assassination on the grounds of family honour does not even reach the courts. In small villages it may be committed without anyone's knowledge and remain a family secret. Happily, the secret of 'illegitimate pregnancy' is also frequently kept by protective mothers and sisters who manage to hide the 'offence' of their sister or daughter by sending her, for example, to visit a relative living far away or to a maternity home, during her pregnancy. As for the medical profession, it has little inclination to collaborate in such matters. Quite the contrary; doctors have frequently turned out to be in collusion with the justice-hungry family, although perfectly aware that by giving a false diagnosis they might have saved two human lives.

Those doctors, scientists and writers who have dared to deal with the subject have been, and still are subjected to the strictest censorship. Such is the case of writer, Yussef Al-Masri, outspoken in his vehement denunciation of the violence inflicted on women in sexual matters. His book, published in France in 1968, is virtually unknown by the Egyptian public.

The same applies to Nawal Al-Saadawi, the author of fourteen works, dealing mainly with the position of women in the Arab world. Daughter of a landed middle-class family, Nawal Al-Saadawi had a traditional upbringing. Her own experience as a Muslim woman and what she heard from the women she has attended and treated throughout her career (her psychiatric practice was in Benha, a large town in the Nile Delta) are the basis of her feminist struggle and of her books. Yet her books have had to be published in Beirut and are not on sale in Egypt, at least not the most recent. Moreover, she has experienced all kinds of setbacks in her professional life. Her outspokeness cost her the positions of Director General to the Ministry of Health and editor of a medical journal. In *Women and Sex* she particularly attacks the taboos surrounding virginity, which are closely connected with female circumcision. On this sensitive subject, I shall borrow some of her observations.

According to Al-Saadawi, speaking of the Arab Middle East, the hymen is the most important part of the female organism. The loss of any other part is less regrettable and is credited with less importance than that of this precious membrane.

Generally speaking, there is complete ignorance regarding organic differences in women. These may range from the absence of a hymen to its relatively greater flexibility or fragility. According to research carried out in 1972 by the Baghdad Institute of Research on a sample of the population, it seems that only 41.32 per cent of women have a 'normal' hymen: 11 per cent of girls are born with very flexible, 16.16 per cent with very fine hymens and 31.32 per cent with hymens that are both flexible and resistant.

Making these facts known would avoid many misunderstandings and spare those girls suspected of 'sinful behaviour' because on their wedding night there is no trace of blood after defloration. It may even happen that the mere practice of a strenuous sport (horse-riding or swimming, for example) in early childhood is in itself enough to cause a rupture of the hymen.

Nawal Al-Saadawi tells just such a story of a young bride who came to her in tears the morning after her wedding night because her husband had renounced her, suspecting that she was not a virgin. The gynaecological examination showed that the young woman had a flexible hymen, whose main characteristic is that it does not bleed at the moment of defloration.

In Egypt and probably in other Arab countries, the practice of premarital medical consultations is unknown, except when the question arises of obtaining a certificate of virginity at the request of a suspicious husband or punctilious relatives. Indeed, the notion of 'honour' is very important. It is not only the honour of the young girl that is stake in the case of a loss of virginity but that of her future husband and her entire family. For the latter, it is a question of not delivering 'second-hand merchandise'.

If this overestimation of the value of virginity is more pronounced in working-class milieus, it nonetheless exists in the middle classes too, even though they scoff at it. Young, Westernised, middle-class Egyptian women have the means to avoid strict family surveillance and, because of this, can allow themselves more freedom; they are not exposed to the repression that affects poorer women. What is more, they have access to the means of giving themselves the appearance of virtue. For them, restoring 'virginity', or resorting to a medically supervised abortion (both expensive operations) is no problem in Egypt, still less abroad.

The only weapon available to working-class women is their own cunning. A few 'old wives' remedies' allow those in need to 'save face'. One of the shrewdest of these consists of inserting into the vagina of the young girl, on her wedding night, a tiny pouch filled with chicken's blood which, at the moment of penetration will gush forth profusely. Another of these 'remedies' consists of arranging that the date of the marriage coincides with that of the bride's period, so as to confuse the husband. Of course, none of these ruses could succeed without the complicity and discretion of the midwife, whose responsibility it is to see that all goes well.

The suffering of the unmarried mother

The unmarried mother has no status whatever in Egypt. Legally, such a situation is non-existent, since the law makes no allowance for it and, furthermore, it is banned by society. When a child is born under such conditions, it is immediately taken from its mother and committed to an institution. Orphanages, mostly run by nuns, take in these children whose maintenance is assumed by Child Welfare.

Adoption is not recognised in Muslim law but it sometimes happens that a wealthy family without descendants gives a home to some child and legitimises it.

During their pregnancy, unmarried mothers may be accepted into centres or hostels run by charitable organisations. An unmarried, pregnant woman is a subject of shame and dishonour to her family. With few exceptions, she will find neither shelter nor protection among her family. On the contrary, she risks from them the most brutal punishment, if not her very life and that of her child.

I visited a hostel for unmarried mothers in Heliopolis, a Cairo suburb. There were about a dozen residents, some occupied with household chores, others with dressmaking – the only training given to these mostly illiterate women and girls. Amongst these mothers-to-be, some had been raped by the employer for whom they had worked as maids, others had had some brief affair in the village. To shield her from family vengeance, a sympathetic female relative (usually the mother or aunt) had managed to put the young woman in touch with the hostel in question.

The mother-to-be is kept there until the birth, protected from all visitors and under the care of a social worker. Afterwards, when her baby has been taken from her, she is usually returned to her family who waste no time in marrying her off. Sometimes these young women are disowned by their families. In such cases, they can stay on in the hostel until they have found new employment or accommodation.

If the young woman repeats the 'offence', she has a second and final chance to return to the hostel. After more than two pregnancies, she is considered beyond help.

The fate of the prostitute

An almost identical fate awaits prostitutes, when they are released from prison. In the Egyptian penal code, prostitution is an offence punishable by imprisonment. It was legally authorised until 1949, when it was officially banned. It was mostly taken up by country girls who had come to Cairo in the hope of finding domestic work there. Many of them, before their plans had even begun to take shape, found themselves approached by pimps the moment they got off the train. Later, when access to education for young women began to be accepted, it was the young students from villages, who, on their arrival in town, were caught in the nets of the pimps.

Today, despite the legal interdiction still in force, prostitution has been officially reinstated for the benefit of rich Arab visitors from the Persian Gulf and a few wealthy Egyptians. It draws on both village girls and those from middle- and lower-middle class backgrounds. However, it involves a form of clandestine prostitution difficult to police and, consequently, to curb, for the girls do not 'walk the streets' like common prostitutes, but are set up in flats, often rented or bought by their rich clients. This is the least of the contradictions that exist in this Islamic country where moral harshness and laxity coexist. Some prostitutes are even temporarily married by their clients.

Not all prostitutes are sheltered from the severe punishment handed out not only by the law but also, indeed especially, by society. It is not uncommon even nowadays to see, in the villages or the working-class districts of the big towns, a woman suspected of adultery or prostitution being dragged through the streets and beaten or flogged, or even having her throat cut.

The two sources of Islamic law, the *Quran* and the *Sunna*, display a strict but limited severity regarding the punishment for illicit traffic in sex, seen as a crime against religion. The *Quran* speaks of one hundred lashes for the guilty party. Furthermore, proof of guilt must be very clearly established, in other words there must be witnesses. According to the *Quran*, bearing false witness is as reprehensible as the offence itself. In the *Quran*, Sura XXIV, the Sura of Light, states:

> Those that defame honourable women and cannot produce four witnesses shall be given eighty lashes. No testimony of theirs shall be admissible, for they are great transgressors.
> You carried with your tongues and uttered what your mouths did not know. You may have thought it a trifle, but in the sight of Allah it was a great offence.
> (*verse 15*)

Such niceties are extremely unlikely to impress the man in the street who reacts impulsively to any threat, even imagined, to strict moral order and decency. But the cruel treatment meted out to those engaged in, or suspected of prostitution is reserved for the poorer women; expensive prostitutes find ways to avoid it.

Officially, a 'rehabilitation' programme for prostitutes was set up by the Ministry of Social Affairs. Since 1960, the law authorises the placing in institutions of 'delinquents' after they have paid their debt to society. This ranges from six months to three years in prison, depending on the seriousness of the offence. In 1972 it was estimated that the success rate of the rehabilitation programme was 35 per cent, 65 per cent of the women concerned having returned to prostitution, and with good reason. In 1979, in the suburbs of Cairo, I visited a centre for the rehabilitation of prostitutes run by the same voluntary team of ladies who also look after the unmarried mothers. The setting: a two-storey house with bare walls, completely devoid of any trace of imagination; dormitories without soul or character, as cold as a hospital day room. For some, the latest arrivals, a mattress on the floor by way of a bed, and an identical uniform for all these young women whose candid gaze had a certain disarming quality. Their sole activity was to attend classes in cutting and sewing.

Most of them were from relatively poor backgrounds. Some had been disowned by their families. Others still received occasional visits from relatives, but going out was utterly forbidden, from the time they arrived at the centre until their reintegration into society. Reintegration is not always an easy matter. Tired of waiting on vague promises of work or the possibility of marriage with some gallant man ready to close his eyes to their dark past, these young women are very often driven back into prostitution because they have no other resources. Under the present circumstances, there is in fact little chance of solving their problems by finding a decent job and acquiring a respectable life. In any case, a prostitute is always branded by her past, unless it has been possible to camouflage it, and society refuses to allow her any other role.

Prostitution remains (in the West, too, incidentally) a subject still concealed beneath a veil of prejudice. This is particularly true in Arab Muslim society, still completely permeated by taboos.

[1]There have since been other conferences and seminars on this subject, notably those organised by the Inter-African Committee in Dakar (1984) and Ethiopia (1987).

7
The Legal Status of Women

Shari'a **Law versus women's emancipation**

In Egypt at present, the overwhelming preoccupation of enlightened opinion is the reform of women's personal status, in other words of the outdated laws governing marriage and divorce. Thanks to pressure brought to bear by progressive circles, a slight improvement in women's status was achieved in June 1979. Already, at the beginning of the century, feminist struggles had become interwoven with those of the nationalist movement, but the history of these struggles is long, confused and contradictory. Indeed, it is incomprehensible without an analysis of the principal Quranic laws that govern Egyptian society. Egypt occupies a privileged place in both the Arab and the Islamic worlds; on its soil stands the mosque and university of Al-Azhar, the accepted authority on matters of Quranic interpretation.

In all Muslim countries, social relationships are governed by Quranic law, the *Shari'a*. The legislation concerning marriage and family life is based on the *suras* of the Quran and the *hadiths* of the *Sunna*. The *Quran*, the Muslim holy book, contains the revelations made by God to the Prophet Mohammed, at the beginning of the seventh century. The Muslim faith is based on this written word. For all practicing Muslims, it is necessary not only to profess this faith, but to live and adhere to it completely, in order to experience the truth.

Islam has 900 million followers in the world. The community in its entirety is called the *Umma*. After the death of the Prophet, in 632 AD, divisions appeared within the Islamic community. Soon, two main factions confronted each other: the *Shiites*, the minority faction, which accounts for around 10 per cent of the entire Muslim community and the *Sunnite*, representing the majority. This split (*firaq*) has its origins in the civil war between the Caliph Ali, cousin and son-in-law of the Prophet, and Moawiya, a relative of Osman and leader of the Ummayyad tribe which, afterwards, determined people's allegiance to one or other of the leaders of the rival factions. Sunnite (or orthodox) Islam itself is divided into four legal schools which disagree on certain points of their interpretation of the *Shari'a*. These schools or creeds are, chronologically: the *Maliki*, the *Hanafi*, the *Shafa'i* and the *Hanbaali*, from the names of the ulemas who founded them, from the middle of the eighth to the middle of the ninth century.

Several *suras* of the *Quran* deal with the position of women, their rights and obligations to society. It must be remembered that, at the time the *Quran* was revealed, women in pre-Islamic Arabia were in the worst possible situation and that the various stipulations laid down by the Quranic law were intended to protect them from total subjection to men and to the clan. In this sense, Islam represented progress when compared to the old customs.

Over the centuries, Islam, which is the most recent of the major monotheistic religions, has had to adapt to the lives of its followers to ensure its survival. Certain governments claiming to be Muslim understood this and reformed their legislation, taking due consideration of reality and their own country's development. Such was the case in Iran, under the Pahlevis, in Turkey under Attaturk, in Tunisia under Bourghiba, and in Morocco at the beginning of the twentieth century.

Although Egypt remains one of the Arab countries where the position of women has been most improved in recent years, there is a great discrepancy between theory and reality. In the sphere of public life, women have acquired maximum rights, almost equal to men. A similar evolution has not taken place in the sphere of private life. Jean-Pierre Peroncel-Hugoz, foreign correspondent for *Le Monde* until 1981, gave a famous example in one of his articles: that of Sadat's ex-Minister of Foreign Affairs, Mme. Aisha Ratib, who, having set out one day on a mission, found her plane stopped just as it was about to leave Cairo airport, because her husband had stepped in to prevent the take-off on the pretext that she had not asked his permission to leave. The law does indeed require a woman wishing to make a journey without her husband to obtain his authorisation. Up until 1979, this authorisation was valid for one year; it has since been extended to five years.

The struggle for women's emancipation began at the start of the nineteenth century and was closely linked to the nationalist struggle from which it was indissociable in the eyes of some patriots. We must bear in mind that, at the time, Egypt was under Franco-British colonial domination, enforced by indigenous local leaders. At this time, a strong, popular resistance movement emerged, mobilising the proletarian and peasant classes. At the same time, a cultural renaissance was spreading, influenced by such thinkers as Gamal Al-Din Al-Afghani and his small group of disciples. In 1855, one of these disciples, Ahmed Faris Al-Shidyak, published *Les Jambes Croisées*, one of the first books favourable to women's emancipation. Another eminent scholar, Rifa'a Al-Tahtawi, chosen by Mohammed Ali to head the first Egyptian cultural mission to France (1823), discovered that, in the West, 'the women are like the men in everything'. Convinced from this moment of the necessity of educating women in order to raise the standard of their lives, he wrote two fundamental books: *A Guide for the Education of Girls and Boys* (1872) and *General Essays on Paris* (1902). Then came Sheikh Mohammed 'Abdu, champion of the nationalist struggle of the *Wafd*, an influential theorist and an ardent supporter of women's rights. He fought for the abolition of concubinage and polygamy, invoking the equality between men and women advocated by Islam.

The fundamental work on the problem of women's emancipation is, however, *Tahrir Al-Mara'a* (Woman's Liberation) published in 1899, by Kassim Amin, a well-known legal writer of Kurdish origin; this was followed, in 1911, by *Al-Mar'a Al-Jedida* (The New Woman). This author's defence of women's rights to education brought upon him the critical thunderbolts of the religious establishment (*Al-Azhar*) as well as that of government circles. Khedive Ismail himself attacked him. He was even condemned by the nationalist opposition and its leader, Mustafa Kamil, who, in 1910, published an article in the newspaper *Al-Liwa*, hostile to Kassim Amin's ideas. Other opponents and champions of women's emancipation – one of the best known of the latter was Taha Hussain – aired the debate in the pages of the press and the literature of the period. Women, too, had joined the ranks of those struggling for their liberation. Amongst them were: Aisha

Al-Taymouria, Zainab Fawwaz, Malaak Hefni Nassif (1886–1918) and Mai Ziyyada (during 1915 the latter held a literary salon in Cairo), all authors of literary works dealing with women's liberation.

Two important periods have marked the history of Egyptian feminism; they correspond to precise critical moments in the history of colonial Egypt. In 1919, women participated *en masse* in the nationalist struggle which the *Wafd* party was waging against British occupation. Urban women workers and village women fought a very real battle to drive out the British. Some lost their lives in the demonstrations and disturbances. Amongst the most famous of martyrs are Shafiqa Mohammed, killed by the British on 14 March 1919, Sayida Hassan, Fahima Ryadh and Aisha Omar. Nawal Al-Saadawi has pointed out the discrepancies between the demands made by the working-class women and peasants and those advanced by the bourgeois women of the period. While the former, living in the most precarious conditions, were asking for the basic minimum necessary to live, women from the ruling classes had concerns which did not directly affect the common women; the wearing of the veil, for example, was enforced only for bourgeois women, not for the proletariat.

The suppression of the veil was, in fact, the major victory of the Egyptian feminist movement which sprang up during the nationalist uprisings of 1919. The Federation of Egyptian Women was founded by a middle-class woman of Turkish origin, Huda Shaarawi. In 1923, she and two of her fellow activists, Cesa Nabarawi and Nabawiya Moussa, also of Turkish origin, succeeded in having the minimum marriageable age for girls raised to sixteen and in ensuring that they should have access to secondary education.

The years 1944 to 1952 also saw the mobilising of progressive women. During this period, the left-wing of the then underground *Wafd* (the party had been banned by the king in 1944), the communists and the independent nationalists had formed a coalition against King Farouk, who was accused of collaborating with imperialism. Militant women took advantage of the prevailing circumstances to draw up a plan to improve the position of women. Amongst the best known were Inji Aflatun, painter, and Doreya Shafik who founded the group *Bint Al-Nil* (Daughter of the Nile), an organisation that fought actively for the reform of women's personal status and their civil rights. Their struggle came up against the opposition of *'ulemas* of Al-Azhar who promptly issued a *fatwa* (legal decree) on 11 June 1952, refusing to grant women the right to vote.

The struggle for women's emancipation had its finest hour in 1952, during the coup of the Free Officers and Nasser's revolution. After the nationalising of the Suez Canal in 1956, and thanks to the new constitution decreed by Nasser the same year, women gained the right to the vote. The law of 7 April 1959 accorded men and women the same legal rights regarding work and, in addition, granted women a series of privileges based on their role as mothers, for example, the right to sick leave on 70 per cent of their normal salary and of working part-time without jeopardising their right to the retirement pension. The Charter of 1962, issued by Nasser, granted women the right of eligibility to work and established the basis of equal pay for equal work for men and women. From this date, it became possible for women to have access to ministerial posts; even today, however, a woman can be neither a governor nor a judge.

Thus, women gradually acquired considerable civil and political rights, yet few women benefited from this. At the beginning of 1979, only four women candidates had been elected to the National Assembly. In June 1979, after the dissolution of this National Assembly and the constitution of a new one, President Sadat reserved thirty seats for women in addition to those they might win in open elections. A few women were appointed to important posts in administration, the press, radio and television.

There would, therefore, appear to have been an emergence of women into public life. But a few women to whom I spoke, all committed intellectuals, expressed their disappointment at the passive and apathetic attitude women evinced toward the problems facing them. In fact, there is a total contradiction between the possibilities offered women by the laws governing work, and the limitations imposed by marriage laws and common law.

At present, women seem less motivated to militant action than they were at the time of Huda Shaarawi and Doreya Shafik. There are no longer any organised feminist groups, neither in university nor elsewhere.* All that remains of Huda Shaarawi's original movement is a tiny nucleus whose activities have been reduced to fashionable philanthropic meetings and charity work.

---

* Since this was written a women's organisation, the Arab Women's Solidarity Association, based in Cairo, has been established.

Why this apathy? Because today women are up against *Shari'a* law. For women in contemporary Egypt, there is an enormous gap between their rights as citizens and their status as private individuals. Regarding their private status, legislation still discriminates against them, and *Shari'a* law, according to '*ulemas'* interpretation, is less than generous or fair with regard to women, particularly in matters of legislation concerning marriage and the family. There was, however, some slight progress in the 1970s, thanks to the 'lobbying' by the Cairo Association of Family Planning and to the vigorous interventions of its then president, Mme. Sadat. In June 1979, as a result of these efforts, the National Assembly adopted a new law on the position of women, with particular bearing on the protection of women who have been 'renounced'; but divorce by mutual consent has still not been achieved, and polygamy still exists. The laws of inheritance still work in favour of the male and to the detriment of the female: the latter has the right to only half the share that each of her brothers receive. The men who devised the law justify this inequality by claiming that it is intended to compensate for the man's obligation to provide for his family. In Egypt today, this argument is no longer valid. Since women gained access to paid work, the man is no longer the family's sole support. Quite the contrary, the extremely low wages paid to their husbands force most working-class women – in the towns at least – to seek work outside the home.

'Marriage is the greater part of religion'
'Better the shadow of a man than the shadow of a wall'

These two popular sayings epitomise the significance of the institution of marriage for Egyptian society. Prescribed by the *Quran*, marriage is considered as a duty by believers:

> Take in marriage those among you who are single and those of your male and female slaves who are honest. If they are poor, Allah will enrich them from His own abundance. Allah is munificent and all-knowing.
> Let those who cannot afford to marry live in continence until Allah enriches them.

Marriage (*al-Nikah*) is regulated by Muslim law (*Shari'a*) which lays down the rights and obligations of husband and wife. In practical terms, Muslim marriage is a contract entered into by the two parties. It is the father, or the woman's legal representative (the *wali*) who signs the marriage contract with the husband. Registration of the contract is required in cases where a previous divorce has to be declared or in the case of remarriage.

In Islam, sexual relations between man and woman are permissible only in marriage. All sexual relations outside marriage, referred to as *zinna* (fornication), are seen as religious interdictions. This prohibition also applies to all forms of sexual contact considered as deviant or perverted, such as homosexuality, sodomy, etc. Thus, every unmarried man or woman stands accused in any extra-marital sexual relationship. In practice, men have no scruples whatever about indulging in *zinna*, whereas the harshest social censure is implacably brought to bear at the discovery of a woman who has 'sinned.'

In Arab society, celibacy is despised. The aim of marriage is to perpetuate the species, therefore to procreate. Only marriage assures the individual of a place in society. An unmarried woman has no social status, with the exception of a few rare women with prestigious careers such as actresses, lawyers, doctors and film-makers, although even they frequently encounter obstacles that with an influential husband they would probably have been spared. Without professional training, without work, an unmarried woman, whatever her age, is reduced to living under her family's protection. Usually, she is assigned the most thankless of household tasks and has almost no contact with the outside world. This need to virtually isolate young, unmarried women doubtless explains the obsessive haste most families display in 'settling' their daughters at any price. Witness the following speech, recorded in Zarka, a little village in the Nile Delta, where the mother of a young bride-to-be of fifteen gleefully told me: 'When Zainab's fiancé came to ask for her and told us how much he earned and what he was going to pay as marriage settlement, I said to him: "Good, you can take her" (*yallah sheel!*).'

Girls are somehow seen as surplus merchandise to be off-loaded as quickly as possible. In working-class circles, this happens particularly in large families where an uneducated girl becomes more of a burden in the home than a help. Thus, she will be handed over, as soon as possible, to the first-comer vaguely capable of providing for her. Admittedly, the alleged sexual precociousness of the oriental woman is not incompatible with such practices. Moreover, the life-style in rural communities – living in close contact with the animal world, the cramped conditions of the houses, the births continually taking place in the home – all combine to open children's eyes very early to matters of love and sex. But this early awakening of the senses is immediately repressed by social restrictions. In contrast, in certain wealthier milieus, the subject of sexuality is surrounded by silence, to the extent that boys and girls – particularly the girls – sometimes come to marriage totally ignorant of sexual matters.

According to an old tradition, a girl of marriageable age who remains unwed is an object of shame and scandal. She arouses in men vague desires and lascivious thoughts. It is, therefore, better that the girl be married at an early age. Early marriages are still very frequent in rural areas, where the proportion of illiterate girls is much higher than in the towns, and despite Egyptian law, which has laid down the minimum age of marriage as sixteen for girls and eighteen for boys. In theory, no marriage can be officially registered unless both parties comply with these regulations. But this obstacle can easily be overcome, especially in rural areas. Very often, neither of the marriage applicants possesses a birth certificate stating their age. In such cases, the *ma'azun* (registrar) will be presented with a certificate giving an approximate age. There is no real control over the work of the *ma'azun*, hence the many infringements of the law. The law raising the age of consent, adopted in 1924, was one of the victories of Huda Shaarawi's movement.

If tradition in rural areas seems unshakeable, it must be admitted that in recent years there have been changes in the towns at all social levels. The rate of school attendance for girls has increased considerably in the last twenty years; also, the current economic climate has need of an expanding female workforce.

In some cases, young women become the main family breadwinner and thus manage to avoid an arranged and unwanted marriage. Furthermore, in Cairo and Alexandria, overpopulation and, by extension, housing problems are becoming acute. Young couples are unable to find flats at prices they can afford. In the rural areas, the young married woman still lives with her mother-in-law, but in towns, young couples prefer their independence. Consequently, plans for early marriage are often discouraged or postponed.

In traditional Arab society, marriage is the most important single event in the life of the individual. The extended family is the norm and notions of solidarity and interventionism are closely linked. It is rare for a boy or girl to escape the consensus of public opinion and, in general, the partner is chosen by the family.

A survey carried out by the National Centre of Research and Criminology reveals that, of the women interviewed, 94.7 per cent of those from rural backgrounds had had their husbands chosen by their family. As for the men, the survey shows that 40 per cent of them had suffered the same fate in rural areas and 24 per cent in urban areas, which gives the following apparently paradoxical, comparative results: in the country, 74 per cent of men had chosen their wives and, in the towns, 53 per cent. The reason for this given by the researchers is that in the village, men have greater freedom of choice because the social unit is more limited and the possibility of meeting and knowing the future spouse is therefore greater. In the town, however, where a communal life-style is less and less possible, such opportunities are much rarer.

This freedom of choice does not work the other way round. On the contrary, girls, seen in the village, in the fields or at festivals, are targets of male lust, without themselves being able to indicate a preference. Worse, both partners are often trapped, because the matter has been settled well in advance. Betrothals arranged by the family rank above personal choice. In the kindergarten of the village of Al-Ghanaiyim, I overheard the father of a five-year-old girl explain that she would be absent because during a fight with her cousin, he had kicked her, justifying his action by pointing out that, after all, she was his fiancée!

The aim of endogamy or inbreeding, still practised – though to a lesser degree since the revolution of 1952 – was to protect the family heritage. To some extent, the agricultural reforms decreed by Nasser's revolution have changed the social structure and thus weakened the rationale for endogamy. Only tradition perpetuates the practice.

Islamic law has, however, imposed certain restrictions on marriage. It is forbidden between blood relatives (lineal consanguinity, phratry, uncles, nephews), between in-laws (mother-, daughter- and sister-in-law). It is also forbidden between a foster-mother and her child, the foster-mother being classed as the natural mother. Marriage between a Muslim man and a Christian or Jewish woman is valid conditional upon the children being brought up as Muslims. In the case of a Muslim woman and a non-Muslim man then the man must convert to Islam.

To retrace the origins of the practice of enforced marriage for girls, a brief historical reminder is necessary: in pre-Islamic Arabia, the situation of women was extremely precarious. Girl babies were sometimes buried alive at birth. Custom decreed that the young girl's father or guardian (*Wali*) arranged her marriage, with or without her consent (according to some sources she was sometimes consulted); this was known as the *jabr*. With the advent of Islam, this notion of constraint was abolished. Islam taken literally is perfectly just and provides for any girl with a normal capacity to make decisions and who is of age to denounce or annul a marriage contract. She should even have the option to do this at a later stage if, at the time of the marriage, she were unable to do so. The considerable gap between legal rules and the way they are put into practice permits abuses of all kinds. Nowadays, the right of *jabr* is invoked against girls of marriageable age who are considered simple-minded or incapable of making a lucid choice. Obviously any illiterate young peasant girl can be made to fit one of these categories. The family has ample scope to oppose the marriage of any girl whose chosen partner it considers unworthy or unsuitable.

One of my Muslim school friends, found herself, at sixteen, engaged to a fiancé she did not want, because she was in love with another young man. Shortly after the marriage, the husband was struck down by mental illness. The family was then forced to accede to the girl's first choice and she was remarried, this time to the man of her choice!

Muslim marriage involves three main steps: the betrothal party (*Al-Khutba*) celebrated with a certain ostentation in all milieus; the signing of the marriage contract (*Katb Al-Kitab*) which involves no ceremony or celebration; the *Dokhla* (the wedding night, properly speaking) which is the occasion for great festivity.

The betrothal party and the signing of the marriage contract can be done by proxy, in other words without either party being present. Nowadays this is increasingly common due to the emigration of so many young men to the Gulf countries in search of employment. The girl's brother is then responsible for representing her absent fiancé. When one of these young men, who may have been abroad for several years in search of steady, well-paid work, is ready to get married, he can even 'order' a wife by post. The commitment made at the betrothal ceremony is seen as a moral obligation. The commitment is sealed by the *Shabka* (the bond) which takes the form of a gift, usually jewellery, which the fiancé offers to his future wife. In the event of the betrothal being broken off by the girl, the *Shabka* is returned. In contrast, when the man breaks off the engagement, his ex-fiancée retains the *Shabka* as compensation. It is also during the betrothal celebration that negotiations take place regarding the amount of the marriage settlement, the *mahr*, which the husband-to-be provides to cover the costs of the trousseau and setting up house. The trousseau is often on show for several weeks for the benefit of the entire neighbourhood: brightly coloured quilts, sheets, cushions covered in taffeta or embroidery are displayed in a room in the family home while waiting for the bride-to-be to move in.

The amount of the *mahr* varies according to the milieu and the financial means of the prospective husband. But the minimum sum payable is twenty-five piastres. The amount is included in the marriage contract and may be paid in two instalments (the initial payment being two-thirds). The contract also includes a clause stipulating that, in the event of a separation, the woman will have the remaining third, in other words, the sum outstanding (*Al-Moakhar*).

The *Katb Al-Kitab*, a ceremony which is both religious and civil, takes place in the presence of two witnesses, one of whom is the *ma'azun* (the registrar) and the other the legal representative of the young woman (*Al-Wali*). Only the registration of the said contract by the *ma'azun* (who also fulfills a religious function) – as we have seen earlier – gives the stamp of authenticity.

A long period may elapse between the *Katb Al-Kitab* and the *Dokhla* (consummation of the marriage). This often occurs, for example, when the man is absent, doing military service or working abroad. In such a situation, the couple is obliged to remain celibate. Only the *Dokhla* allows the couple to cohabit. In rural areas this event is celebrated by the entire village which participates in the festivities. The Jesuit Father, Henri Ayrout, who lived for many years in the villages of Upper Egypt and worked for their improvement, described these celebrations in his book *Fellahs of Egypt*:

On the wedding day, in other words the day when the bride leaves her father's house for that of the groom, all her belongings are loaded on to a couple of camels rented for the occasion and paraded through the village. Young girls walk before and behind them, singing and clapping their hands and the good people admire the riches marching past. This is in the afternoon. Then the wedding feast is carried past in procession on huge plates, from the bride's house to the bridegroom's. Finally comes the bride's farewell tour of the village. The previous day, the village matrons have bathed and washed her; her hands and feet have been decorated with henna.

The procession forms. The bride, on the back of a camel or in an ancient car smothered in flowers, is hidden beneath red or white fabric. Two or three relatives are with her under this canopy.

Men fire rifle-shots into the air (the Arab influence), while the *zagharits* (high pitched trilling) and the singing of the women alternate. The groom is also prepared. His comrades surround him with candles and a torch-lit procession is organised. He carries a white handkerchief which he holds up to his face, like a mask. Finally, they reach the house. The groom's friends tear him away from the crowd and drag him inside. Alone, he enters the wedding chamber. The young bride is already there, surrounded by female relatives from both families. In the most primitive manner, they will verify her virginity. The blood flows . . . she cries out. Her cry is taken up outside in the trilling cries of the women and the joyous rifle shots of the men. Honour is now safe. Now the festivities begin; they will last until dawn, very noisy but always the men and women separate; to each their rejoicing. On such an occasion, no expense is spared. Late into the night, with little secrecy, the marriage will be consummated. For a week the new husband will do no manual work.

Polygamy

If you fear you cannot treat orphans with fairness, then you may marry other women who seem good to you: two, three or four of them, but if you fear you cannot maintain equality among them, marry one only or any slave-girls you may own. This will make it easier for you to avoid injustice.
Quran, Sura IV, verse 3

Is this Quranic verse a justification of polygamy? It must be remembered that in pre-Islamic Arabia, polygamy was widespread and the number of wives taken was unlimited. Furthermore polygamy was not confined to the Arabs; it was already practised by the Hebrews, the Sicilians, the Saxon tribes and the Egyptian Pharaohs.

Looking closely at Quranic texts and placing them in their historical context, it can be seen that on the one hand, each directive has its justification in a given sociological and historic situation, and on the other hand, they are all of a repressive nature. Thus, the Quranic verse authorising polygamy has its origin in a historic event, the defeat of Ohod, in 625, which created numerous widows in Arabia following the deaths of so many husbands and fathers. This same verse is followed by a second which hastens to qualify the first by implicitly condemning polygamy, on the grounds that the state of perfect equality is humanly unattainable:

> Try as you may, you cannot treat all your wives impartially. Do not set yourself together against any of them, leaving her, as it were, in suspense. If you do what is right and guard yourself against evil, you will find Allah forgiving and merciful.
> *Quran*, Sura IV, verse 129

If Islam has not abolished polygamy, it has theoretically made it more difficult to practise by laying down as a condition, complete equality between the different wives. In limiting the number of wives to four, the *Quran*, though it may seem extremely generous, is actually making the practice of polygamy more difficult. It is already no easy matter to be fair to two wives, still less to four! In general, however, men who practise polygamy do not possess an extensive knowledge of Quranic interpretaton. With a little help from masculine hypocrisy, this authorisation simply means unscrupulous abuse of the right to have more than one wife.

While female adultery is a punishable offence, it is legally permitted for the man. On this score, supporters of polygamy resort to various justifications of a religious, moral, economic or social nature. The most commonly cited is that of an innate polygamous instinct in the male. Reference is also made to the hypocrisy of Judeo-Christian societies where concubinage and polygamy are often practised in secret. Other reasons have been put forward by *Shari'a* law to justify polygamy. These have to do with very specific situations and circumstances, such as sterility or mental illness in the first wife, or a surplus of women following a war. It is alleged that polygamy prevents divorce. The man, in his magnanimity and generosity, rather than rid himself of a wife he no longer wants, bestows on her the honour and privilege of sharing her home with another!

Due to a self-imposed ban on repudiating any of his wives, the Prophet Mohammed himself acquired a total of eight wives, and this without counting his twenty or so concubines. This precedent is often cited but it is not accepted by Islamic scholars, for the Prophet and his wives are seen as a special case. In the context of the period, he was obliged, for political and tribal reasons, to take various wives. The latter no doubt chose to stay with him rather than be reduced to solitude and chastity, since they were not allowed to remarry (later being repudiated), in compliance with the Quranic injunction:

> You must not speak ill of Allah's apostle, nor shall you ever wed his wives after him; this would be a grave offence in the sight of Allah.
>
> *Quran*, Sura XXXIII, verse 53, al 3

Polygamy, however, is not unanimously accepted, either in the Arab world or in Egypt itself. Certain Islamic countries (notably Morocco and Syria) have taken strict measures to control it. In Egypt, various committees fighting to improve women's situation are tackling the problem. But, so far, there is still no law forbidding it. Yet there is no lack of arguments against it: first and foremost, the jealousy of the wives and the injustices and traumas this causes the children; polygamy is also responsible for the increase in the birthrate. Obviously, as long as a woman's value is measured by her capacity to bear children, rivalry will force each wife to compete with the others by having more children.

The following tables give the results of a survey on polygamy in Egypt undertaken by the Central Agency for the Diffusion of Statistics.* From a population of around 33 million, in 1970, it was estimated there were 24,283 (i.e. around 9 per cent) polygamous

---

*Statistics of marriage and divorce (publ. No. 1-1214, 1972) published in Vol. 11 of the journal of the National Centre of Social Research and Criminology in Cairo, under the title: *Law and Population Project in Egypt*, 1975.

marriages. Tables 1, 2, 3 and 5 are based on limited samples: 600 families in urban areas and 300 families in rural areas. (The inequality of the samples was deliberate because of greater diversification in the urban area as opposed to the more homogeneous rural area.)

Table 1
Comparative table of polygamy and monogamy in rural and urban areas

Category	Rural Areas Numbers	%	Urban Areas Numbers	%
Polygamy	31	10.4	32	5.3
Monogamy	269	89.6	568	94.7
Total	300	100%	600	100%

From Table 1 it is immediately obvious that the rate of polygamy is twice as high in rural areas as in urban.

Table 2
Grades of income of polygamous husbands in rural and urban areas (according to sample interviewed)

Monthly income in £ Egyptian	Rural Areas % of polygamous spouses	Urban areas % of polygamous spouses
Less than 10	38.4	–
10–19	45.6	25
20–29	12.8	15.6
30–39	3.2	22
40–49	–	18.7
50–59	–	18.7
Total	100%	100%

It is interesting to note the link between polygamy and low incomes in the rural areas, whereas in urban areas the incomes of polygamous husbands are higher.

Table 3
Professional categories of polygamous husbands

Professions	Rural Area %	Urban Area %
Civil servants	9.7	40.6
Liberal professions	–	25
Tradesmen	6.4	9.4
Industrial workers	6.4	6.3
Public sector workers	9.7	6.3
Agricultural workers	9.7	–
Landowners	–	–
Peasants owning or renting less than 5 feddans	48.4	–
Peasants owning or renting 5 to 10 feddans	6.5	–
Peasants owning or renting 15 to 20 feddans	3.2	–
Peasants owning or renting more than 20 feddans	–	–
Without profession	–	12.4
Total	*100%*	*100%*

Table 3 shows that the highest percentage of polygamous men (48.4%) in the rural areas are peasants possessing or renting less than five feddans of land; in urban areas the highest percentage (40.6%) are civil servants.

Table 4
Categories of married men classified according to their educational level, in relation to the number of spouses dependent on them[1]

Educational Level	No. of Dependent Spouses			
	1	2	3	Total
Illiterate	10,303	496	45	10,844
Reading only	670	25	1	696
Literate (able to read and write)	11,096	443	41	11,580
Certificate of business studies	680	15	1	696
Higher certificate of business studies	97	–	1	98
University degree or specialised college	337	3	–	340
Doctorate	7	–	–	7
Not known	22	–	–	22
Total	23,212	982	89	24,283

[1] According to statistics recorded in 1970. Official censuses take place, since 1966, every ten years. The figures are therefore approximate.

According to Table 4 the relationship between polygamy and educational level is one of inverse proportion. The figures obtained show a much greater number of polygamous men among the illiterate and those with only basic schooling than amongst those with university education.

Table 5
Husbands classified according to their educational level, related to the number of wives dependant on them, in rural and urban areas (according to the sample chosen)

Education Level	Rural Areas		Urban Areas	
	1 wife %	2 wives %	1 wife %	2 wives %
Illiterate	68.1	96.7	26.8	30
Recently literate	29.1	3.3	28.3	30
Primary school certificate	0.4	–	11.1	–
Pre-school only	0.4	–	3.8	–
Certificate of business studies	1.5	–	11.4	15
Higher certificate of business studies	–	–	4.3	10
University degree or doctorate	0.5	–	14.3	15
Total	100%	100%	100%	100%

Table 5 confirms that the rate of polygamy is very high among the uneducated in rural areas, and much less so in urban areas.

On the question of whether to maintain or abolish polygamy, only men were consulted by the researchers. In the rural areas, 60 per cent of them were in favour of maintaining polygamy, and only 30 per cent of abolishing it. In the urban areas, the proportions were reversed, 66.7 per cent of those interviewed being in favour of abolishing it and 33.4 per cent of maintaining it. The main findings that emerge from this survey make it clear that polygamy and the ideology that justifies it are more common in rural areas than urban. This is readily understandable: in the more traditional milieu, men are extremely attached to their prerogatives. The rural life-style has remained largely communal; the habitat, the lack of intellectual and social mobility combined with the geographical isolation mean that the rural areas are much more likely than the towns to preserve the ideology and practical application of polygamy. In towns, on the other hand, the rise in the cost of living, the acute housing crisis and a general modernisation have led to a certain indifference and a gradual decrease in the practice of polygamy.

Divorce 'Egyptian style'

A polygamous bus driver brought off an extraordinary 'double' on Sunday when he formally renounced his two wives, one after the other, between bus stops, to the delight of his passengers. The driver of the bus, which was on the 'Ataba-Giza run, had brought his second, and newest wife to keep him company during the interminable traffic jams in central Cairo. At the first stop, he had the nasty shock of seeing his first wife board the bus, accompanied by her mother. The three women quickly transformed the bus into a battle field, and neither the driver nor the other passengers could subdue these three furies. Unanimously supported by his passengers, the bus driver therefore stopped his vehicle outside the first *ma'azun's* office they came to and returned to the wheel a few minutes later having renounced his two wives. His return was greeted by a standing ovation.

This news item, albeit told in an anecdotal style, is a rather crude but nonetheless truthful example of the everyday reality experienced by many women in Islam. The most common form of divorce acknowledged by Islamic law is the *talik*, or one-sided repudiation of the wife by the husband. Such renunciation can be either revocable or definitive. Generally speaking, the man has only to pronounce three times the phrase *anti talik* (you are renounced) before a witness. The divorce comes into effect, according to the *Sunna*, only after a time lapse corresponding to three menstrual cycles of the woman, or if she is pregnant, after the birth. During this period, called the *idda*, an over-hasty or repentant husband can at any time – with or without his wife's consent – go back to living with her. After this new attempt to live together, the husband may, if he wishes, use exactly the same procedure to renounce his wife a second time and submit her to another wait of three months if he sees fit. If this second attempt also ends in failure, the divorce becomes irrevocable.

Various interpretations have been worked out by Islamic legal experts regarding Quranic law's basic principle recognising the man's right to renounce his wife. Using such interpretations, Egyptian jurisprudence has expressed certain reservations and has also made provision for the woman to seek divorce under certain limited, specific circumstances:

– Non-consummation of the marriage due to impotence or other sexual problems.

– Failure on the part of the man to provide for the woman.

– Incurable illness in the man.

– Moral or physical harm done to the woman by the man.

– Prolonged absence by the husband.

– Imprisonment of the husband for a lengthy period.

In such cases, it is the court that grants the decree at the woman's request. As we have seen earlier, this same law allows the insertion the in the marriage contract of a special, optional clause, called the *Isma*; if it is included in the marriage contract, it gives the woman as well as the man the right to seek a divorce. The majority of women, however, although aware of this, do not take advantage of it. From fear of displeasing or even losing their future husband, from lack of foresight, fear of gossip, or simply through their acceptance of what has always been presented to them as a male prerogative, many women fall into the trap. Countless other women are not even informed of the existence of the *Isma*.

Following is a brief history of the mostly unsuccessful attempts to end the discrimination against women in legal matters concerning marriage and domestic life.

In 1929, two motions concerning the reform of women's personal status submitted to the parliament headed by Saad Zaghloul were defeated. These motions were taken up again in 1945 and restated. They stipulated that no polygamous marriage would be legal unless registered before a judge. Furthermore, the judge should not agree to register such a marriage without previously having carried out an in-depth inquiry into the character and means of the applicant, in order to establish his ability to guarantee the security and maintenance of his various families.

Even Nasser was unable to bring about any major changes to the famous personal status laws! After the revolution of 1952, the first comprehensive bill liberalising women's status was rejected because of fierce opposition from one of the Free Officers, Salah Salim, who was afraid of offending the religious feelings of Sudanese Muslims and of alienating a large part of the peasant population.

The battle for equality in the law between men and women experienced serious setbacks at the beginning of the 1970s, with the rise of fundamentalism. In 1975, 100 Members of Parliament (a quarter of parliament) called for the reinstatement of *Shari'a* as Egypt's sole law, trying in this way to abolish with one stroke nearly 60 years of secular victories. The proposal was turned down, but the tide of public feeling in the country continued to turn against women.

Anwar Al-Sadat, who came to power after Nasser's death in September 1970, was personally well-disposed towards women's liberation through the influence of his wife, Jihan. To advance matters, he resorted to cunning: when Parliament was dissolved, at the beginning of summer 1979, the President took advantage of the interim period preceding the next elections to issue a decree approving and amending the law of 1929, in favour of the proposals mentioned above. Now, during a parliamentary interim period, presidential decrees have the force of law.

What is the substance of this timid reform and what did Sadat's new personal status law really mean for women? These innovations were aimed at protecting women and children from the all too frequent abuses men commit, by virtue of the freedom accorded them in their capacity as head of the family. Polygamy being allowed under *Shari'a* law, it has become the man's established right, without the other wife, or wives, being able to challenge it. Sometimes, they are even left in ignorance of their husband's second marriage, which can complicate matters when it comes to sharing out the inheritance in the case of the husband dying first.

Under the new law, the husband is obliged to inform the *ma'azun* of the number of his marriages. For his part, the *ma'azun* must notify each of the wives of the state of affairs. Furthermore, the husband's remarriage gives the wife the right to obtain a divorce, providing she seeks it within a year of the day she learned of the marriage. When this period is over, she loses her right.

The man still retains his right to renounce his wife even in her absence. Now, however, he is obliged to notify her of the act of renunciation by registered mail. In the past, it sometimes happened that this document was deliberately sent by 'absconding' husbands to the wrong address. In this way, the woman, who had not received the information in time, lost her right to alimony, which must be applied for within a month of this notification. Such malpractices are now punishable by law and, one hopes, can no longer be committed so easily.

Apart from alimony, which must be paid to her for one year, any wife who is renounced through no fault of her own receives, as compensation, a sum equivalent to two years alimony. In cases of non-payment by the husband, the alimony debt is covered by the State Bank which gives advances on the alimony which it later undertakes to recover from the husband.

Concerning the custody of the children, a few changes have also been made. From now on, the children of a divorced couple are placed in their mother's care; boys until the age of fifteen, girls until marriage, depending on the judge's discretion. Previously, boys stayed with their mothers until the age of seven and girls until the age of ten.

Furthermore, the husband must give up the family home to his ex-wife as long as she has custody of the children. If this is impossible, he must offer her suitable alternative accommodation. This arrangement represents a certain progress when compared to the previous practice where the renounced wife was often cast off with the bare minimum (a bed, one or two saucepans!) or simply thrown into the street.

The humiliating practice of *Beit Al-Ta'a* (house of disobedience), however, has still not been abolished in Egypt. This authorises the man to bring home, under police escort, a wife who has run away to seek shelter elsewhere, with relatives for instance. Whatever the reasons for her flight, should the woman refuse to return to her husband, she is considered by law to be *Nashiz* (pariah or outcast).

Sadat's reform, as we can see, aimed above all to guarantee financial security to the family in general, and to the children in particular. Such security is denied to women without children or to those whose children are no longer in their custody. It would be more accurate, in fact, to see them as preventative measures rather than real reforms of women's status. Yet even these slender gains have raised a storm of protest in Egyptian conservative circles. For the time being, it is out of the question to push matters further. Thus, the plan aimed at creating a situation where divorce is pronounced by a court of law is not even under discussion. This plan, already advocated at the beginning of the century by Sheikh Abdu, envisaged a legal procedure in two phases, comprising first, an attempt by the judge to reconcile the couple; and second, the official pronouncement of the divorce by the same judge and not by the *ma'azun*. In retaliation to this, the religious authorities (the *'ulemas*) already extremely reluctant to introduce the least reform in the personal status of women, claim that domestic problems should be solved within the family circle and not in a court of law. Divorce, with very rare exceptions, therefore remains within the exclusive jurisdiction of the *'ulemas* and the *ma'azun* (registrars administering the *Shari'a*).

8
Future Prospects

In this book, it is the women of Egypt who speak. Women from all walks of life, belonging to the two major religious groups practising in Egypt, Sunnite Muslim and Coptic Christian. These women have shared with us a part of their everyday lives, their desires, fears, joys and suffering, and their constant anxiety to conform to the law.

To whichever of the two major religious groups they belong, they must all bear the constrictive burden of social prejudices and taboos surrounding emotional and sexual life. Mercilessly, the unwritten law compels all of them to wear its repressive shackles. Hind, while she was an unmarried mother, would never have dared return to the village of her birth. Had she done so, she would have suffered the most severe punishment, so great is her crime in the eyes of village society. Aleya and Amina, who share the same husband, do not question the social order established by Mahmoud, although he has made them slaves, exclusively serving his own well-being and pleasure. And so many others, to whom I spoke, all consenting victims to an inhuman system . . .

The taboos and prejudices that oppress all these women have their roots as much in Judeo-Christian civilisation as in the Muslim faith. In a country where both systems are in such close contact, the interaction between them is inevitably intense. However, Islam, the religion of the majority of the population, exercises a predominant influence on Egypt. The legislation inspired by it, *Shari'a* law, is mainly – but not exclusively – responsible for the social, emotional and economic oppression of women.

Egypt is an infinitely complex society. It was the cradle of one of the earliest and most magnificent civilisations in history. It has been the prey of colonial powers. Today, Cairo is the capital of both the Arab and Islamic worlds. But, the most advanced country in the Arab world in terms of industrial development and cultural expression, Egypt is paradoxically one of the most backward in matters of civil legislation. In this country, tradition and modernity clash and mingle inextricably. It is particularly in towns and amongst women engaged in professional training or work that this clash is most intensely felt. In the towns, modernity is symbolised by a system of moral values, by fashions, behaviour and by Western-influenced social practices. But these values, fashions and practices do not readily adapt to the socio-economic reality of recent years. Most women from lower-middle and working-class backgrounds encounter immense difficulties in their daily lives. Poverty and privation, both constantly on the increase, dramatically reduce the possibility of economic emancipation for most women. Poverty is destroying the structure and cohesion of the Arab family as an institution, putting great stress on the traditional solidarity between members of the same clan and resulting in an acute identity crisis for women.

Does Islamic fundamentalism offer a solution to this crisis? It is extremely unlikely. Islamic fundamentalism, a recent phenomenon common to the entire Arab world, is making giant strides in Egypt. Through its rejection of the West, it has acquired the aura of a liberating patriotic force and become a symbol of resistance, of rupture with foreign influence. In proposing a return to Islam's basic structures, Islamic fundamentalism meets the approval of a great many women who, as we have seen, fearful of change, shelter behind traditional values. But fundamentalist ideology asks women to be even more subservient to the dictates of men. Fundamentalist Islam condemns woman's personal emancipation (sexual, emotional, economic and political) as an aberration.

A new interpretation of the *Quran*, obscurantist, repressive and hostile to women, is currently gaining credence among the sheikhs, the legal scholars and their followers. Thus, the net is tightening around women, increasing their isolation from society. The return of the veil, the segregation of the sexes, the ruthless rejection of modernity, are all symptoms of a regression which has for so long been opposed by feminist and avant-garde movements in Egypt. Today, such symptoms are multiplying at a frightening rate.

Concurrently, economic underdevelopment is also becoming daily more accentuated. Since Nasser's death, in September 1970, and more specifically since the War of Ramadan, in October 1973, Egypt has been going through a 'restoration' period: the old ruling classes, the pashas, the big landowners, the urban upper classes, the bankers, merchants and speculators of all kinds, chased out by Nasser, were quickly recalled by Sadat. This economic liberalism, started by Sadat and continued by Mubarak, has so far benefited only a tiny minority of *nouveaux riches*. While huge fortunes are being amassed, the peasants and working class suffer from the constant increase in the cost of living. The suburban female work-forces of Cairo, Alexandria, Assyut and Damietta, the wives, mothers and daughters of the peasants and agricultural labourers of the Delta and Upper Egypt, all suffer directly, they and their families, the disastrous consequences of this so-called free market policy.

Despite such discouraging facts, what strikes me most about Egyptian women is their extraordinary vitality, their capacity to cope with the most difficult situations, their endurance and the apparent serenity with which they face the problems of their everyday existence. This existence is characterised by a profound contradiction: a traditional, 1,000-year-old society has assigned them rigid, unchangeable roles. Yet, however inhuman and discriminatory they may be, these roles give meaning to their lives and the strength to face, day after day, a miserable life with no apparent solution. When all is said and done, however, the situation experienced by the majority of women from the villages and working-class districts of Upper and Lower Egypt is intolerable. This situation is plagued by unhealthy living conditions, poverty – for the poorest – humiliation and discrimination. For most of these women, male autocracy has meant an absence of emotional freedom and of economic and sexual autonomy. All of which makes it impossible for them to exercise their political rights.

What did I hope to bring to all these women who had welcomed me, taught me, who had shared with me their joy and their despair? Could I provoke a questioning of their existence simply by being there amongst them, asking my questions? That would have been very presumptuous on my part. With hindsight, I am aware of a certain lack of tact in my approach. The questions I asked sprang from a preconceived notion: 'You are oppressed, submissive women. Why don't you revolt?' It is with relief that I now realise that none of my questions were able to sow doubts in the minds of the women I spoke to, so unshakeable are their beliefs and their roots in the soil of Egypt. They conform to a tradition, and constantly recreate a pattern of life that serves them as an unchanging point of reference: the pattern constituted by the lives of their mothers, their grandmothers and their entire line since time immemorial. At the same time, I now understand and accept my own mother's attitude faced with a way of life which I saw as 'resigned' and 'backward'. In her lifetime, I often opposed her way of thinking, so different from mine, causing violent clashes! But nothing could dissuade her from a system of values solidly anchored within her. I realise now that she would have been profoundly disoriented if she had been forced to question these values, inherited from generations of women, of which she was the proud bearer.

Is it then premature to hope for a change in the situation of these women isolated in the ghettos epitomised by rural society and the slums of Egypt's big towns? I think not. I remain convinced that Fatma, Messèda, Um Hani, Hind and all the others are the victims of an unfair society, of a mentality still permeated by crippling taboos and obscurantist prejudices. If, in publishing this book, I can contribute to the protracted recognition of this and to the gradual liberation of my sisters in Egypt, the years of work, of travel, of thought, will not have been in vain.

Already, a few women – at the cost of extraordinary efforts – are emerging from the great mass of women in the shadows. A more extensive education system and easier access to a professional career will gradually improve this situation: the numbers of these avant-garde women, still infinitesimal, will increase. Let us hope that this tiny nucleus of liberated women can once more mobilise to help raise the consciousness and bring about an improvement in the situation of all Egyptian women.

I would like to end this book on a personal note. Since this research into the situation of the Egyptian women was motivated by a double purpose – militant and didactic – I take this opportunity to make a few observations linked to my own position as a woman, at the cross-roads between two opposing cultural worlds, the occidental and oriental.

In spotlighting the lives of the women who people my book, I lived through a process of identification. I finally regained the name, the face, the identity which belong to me. During the work, I was constantly, though often unconsciously, drawing parallels between the destinies of the women to whom I was talking and my own. Meeting those who for me had been for so long, shadows of a buried past, awoke emotions, stirred reactions, brought to the surface forgotten patterns of behaviour, repressed since my arrival in the West. In these women I saw my own reflection. I discovered in the destinies of Fatma, Suad and Hind similarities and affinities with my own. True, my route has been different from theirs. In the West, little by little, I have gradually gained everything that can make of me a liberated woman: financial independence, the freedom to make choices regarding my own body, ample contact with the outside world and the means to claim my rights as a woman and as a citizen. But I now realise that in many ways I am still profoundly bound up with my old 'primary', rigid patterns of behaviour, the results of a crippling upbringing, conformist and conservative, which, to this day, is still what the vast majority of Egyptian women undergo. Achieving autonomy, the total liberation of my female being is still my ambition. But, each time I take a step in that direction, an obstructive mechanism intervenes: hesitation and a sort of paralysing fear prevent me from proceeding.

When taking final stock, I yield to the facts: like Fatma, Marsa, Suad and Soraya, I too am a product of the society, the history and the culture which were instilled in me. Indoctrinated by my society from childhood, I had accepted its evaluation of me, submitted to its condemnation. I realise now that I still have not achieved the necessary distance to refute its values, which I criticise violently, but of which I remain the victim, with my own consent and cowardly complicity.

Faced with the women in Egypt I felt, from time to time, contradictory feelings. In way, I envied their fates. A nostalgia for the 'simple life' they lead engulfed me. They at least do not know the anguish of making decisions, of freedom! Baking the bread, looking after the cattle (in the case of the peasants), serving their husband, giving birth to children and bringing them up are their only ambitions. They accomplish them without resentment. For them, there are no contradictions, no painful conflicts between domestic and emotional life, between a professional career, financial autonomy and personal emancipation. At such times, a sudden desire to exchange places came over me. At other times I was seized with a desire to flee, to abandon the research I had undertaken which had forced me to temporarily give up my familiar world in Europe. Alone, far from those closest to me, I had a feeling of sadness, of unbearable loneliness.

I was ready to give up all my intellectual ambitions to return to the security of my family circle. This ambivalence is still with me today.

I am grateful to my Egyptian sisters for having allowed me to compare my life to theirs and, thus, to explore the forgotten dimensions of my being. Thanks to the generosity of their welcome, to their trust in me, to their unstinting hospitality, to the complicity which grew up between us, I was able to share their space. There, I rediscovered the part of me which I had forgotten. In future, I shall assume the responsibility of belonging to these two contradictory, conflicting worlds, the Occidental and the Oriental. Both enthral me, mould me. This double sense of belonging, which I have long experienced as a painful estrangement, now seems to me – thanks mainly to my stay amongst the women of Egypt – a unique opportunity, rich in all the possibilities acquired through the simultaneous participation in two cultures which, though foreign to each other, are both nourished by the immemorial experience of two peoples.

Index